THE HORMONE RESET DIET:

100 DELICIOUS RECIPES TO HELP YOU RESET YOUR HORMONES AND LOSE WEIGHT FAST.

Table of Contents

CHICKEN & POULTRY RECIPES   49

BEEF, PORK, AND LAMB RECIPES   62

FISH AND SEAFOOD RECIPES   76

4

Introduction

The Hormone reset diet is a way for you to reset your body so that you are able to burn fat and have all of the energy that you need. Many people struggle with losing weight, they try starving themselves and exercising until they cannot move. They may start off strong losing a little bit of weight even 10 pounds or so, then their body refuses to lose anymore.

The idea behind the hormone reset diet is that it is because of unbalanced hormones that you are not able to lose the weight. Hormones are actually responsible for a lot of different functions in our bodies and can cause many different problems.

Hormones are what controls how our body reacts to the outside world as well as how our body reacts to food. If your hormones are out of balance then you may struggle with dealing with stress, getting enough sleep, and struggle getting the exercise that your body needs.

Hormones also play a significant role in how your metabolism is functioning as well. They determine how your body uses the food that you eat, whether it is stored for later use, where it is stored, when you feel hungry as well as how much it takes to make you feel full or if you even feel full, whether or not you crave certain foods, as well as how much motivation that you have.

Yes, you read that right, hormones even determine the amount of motivation that you have on any given day. That means that it may not really be your fault that you are not motivated to get up off of the couch and exercise. It could also mean that unlike what we have always been told those cravings were not a lack of willpower but due to unbalanced hormones.

The problem is that since everyone's resting and exercising hormone levels are different you can't just go to the doctor and find out if the reason you are struggling with weight loss is due to an imbalance in hormone levels. Most people's first reaction when they hear that they could be suffering from a hormone imbalance is to run to the doctor in order to get them checked, but the problem with that is that this usually is not a medical issue.

The majority of the time, the reason that your hormones are not balanced is because of a nutritional issue. Our bodies were made to eat specific foods and we live in a time where most people are not eating these types of food, but instead eat food that was made in a lab by scientists. The basics of the hormone reset diet are that you are going to be resetting your body by using the foods that our bodies were made to use as a fuel.

The great thing about hormones is that they give us signals if they are not balanced. We can feel the signals within our body. In order to track the metabolic effect of the body we need to pay attention to three things that we can feel within our body. They are energy, hunger and cravings. By using these three signals that your body is giving you, you will be able to determine if your hormones are the reason that you have not been able to lose weight and keep it off. No matter how hard you try and no matter what you do, you will not be able to lose weight and keep it off if your hormones are not balanced. So before you ever start this diet you are going to have to begin by tracking your hunger, cravings and your energy levels.

Start by getting a notebook and using one sheet of paper for each day. You will want to begin recording your hunger, cravings and energy level several times a day (I recommend hourly) on a scale of 0 to 10. What you want to learn from this is if there are specific times throughout your day when your hunger or craving level is high and your energy level is low.

One example of this may be that you are extremely hungry at 4:30PM right before you get ready to make dinner and your energy levels are low. This could cause you to eat not so healthy foods as well and it is just important to know this information.

If you find that you are experiencing a lot of times when your hunger or craving level is high and your energy level is low, then you will want to go through the entire hormone reset diet. The hormone reset diet is going to help you deal with stress better, sleep better, have more energy and lose weight.

If you find that you are still experiencing a lot of cravings, lacking energy, hungry all of the time, unable to handle stress and not getting restful sleep after you have gone through this diet, then it is time for you to go to your doctor and get a thyroid panel done.

It is important that you do not immediately jump to the idea that there is something that is wrong with your thyroid or adrenal gland, but if you have worked through this diet, are eating healthy, hydrated and getting enough exercise but still not losing weight it is important for you to talk to your doctor about this.

The problem with going to your doctor because you are struggling to lose weight is that they are going to tell you what they have learned and that is that you should restrict the number of calories that you take in each day and burn more. If you keep track of your diet, track what you are eating, drinking and how much you are exercising you will be able to show this to your doctor so that they understand you really are doing everything that you should be doing.

I will be honest, many people think that they are doing what they need to do in order to lose weight but when they put it down on paper they find that they are in fact not doing what they should be. You see, unless you are writing down everything that you are eating and drinking it is easy to forget those little snacks that you had or that cup of coffee with full fat creamer, lots of sugar and whipped cream on top.

The point is that if you can honestly look at your diet journal and know that you have done everything possible to live a healthy lifestyle, but still are not losing weight then you should go and discuss the issue with a doctor.

What is Hormone Reset Diet?

There are many types of diet around! So many, in fact, that you do not know which ones to believe in and actually practice. You can even find some that are all over the World Wide Web, while some are being profusely shoved to your face by either one of your relatives or friends.

Why so many, anyway? What's the difference? Is it because a diet is different for every person? We all have the same kind of system, and the only difference is the proportion and lifestyle for each and every one.

Why can't we just have one sort of diet that can address everybody's problem with just a little tweak for personalization every now and then? Kind of like a skeleton key for a hundred room mansion. Handy, right?

This scenario shouldn't be new to you anymore. You know how dieting starts. The usual drill takes place, you check the internet and review a kind of diet that you heard from a friend who swears to its effectiveness.

You, then, seek for an insight through the help of family, friends, articles or books. If it convinces you well enough, you go to a physician who will help you out with the bits and pieces. He or she will also tailor the diet to fit your lifestyle, weight, and age.

It may seem complete to you, but not really. You are missing something that is a vital factor in your diet and long term health. While you were going through the details of your diet with your physician, did he or she even bothered to check your hormone levels?

"Hormone levels? What for? "That might be the question running in your mind currently. Just so you know, hormones are the ones responsible for keeping your body's ability to combat stress, have great sex, gain fat or muscles and keep them all at an optimal level.

This is not something that would come from your physician through his or her own initiative. Do not expect the same with your dietitian either. Hormones will get into the topic only if you ask your doctor for it or you consult one who specializes in hormones. Asking for tests done to determine your hormone levels would even lead your physician to wonder why you are asking for it.

Do you realize now how sneaky hormones are?

With your hormones, all over the place, do not be surprised if you are not feeling the changes. They are sneaky little ninjas thriving in your body. Either sneaky to your advantage, or against you or most likely, it is the latter. You wouldn't notice the changes in your hormones until you are seriously losing sleep, miserably fat, deeply stressed and you do not know where it all started.

If you cannot find out the source of your failed diet, chances are, it's your hormones trying to let their existence known to you. Think of hormone optimization as the mother of all kinds of diet. Big role, isn't it?

Imagine exercising, eating, pushing yourself to the limits just to attain the right kind of discipline in making your diet a part of your lifestyle. Afterwards, you will find out that you lost only a few pounds or your whole diet failed miserably.

You would end up thinking, "Maybe I do not have enough discipline, yet." So you go ahead and try again. Still, you failed. Spare yourself from these unnecessary heartbreaks. If a diet is not working for you after a lot of honest hard work, don't you think it is time to take a pause and find out what really is going on under the hood?

Before the whole repeated failure pushes you to the limits and leads you to stop the diet thing altogether, let me tell you what is going on. Your hormones are not balanced. Either that or you really have a problem with discipline. However, you know for yourself when you have already tried your best and used up all the resources possible. If you have tried hard enough and your diet is still not working for you when it should have long ago, it is time to stop what you are doing and examine yourself.

No, do not settle for another strange-named diet. Most likely, if your hormones are not balanced, trying another sort of diet would still end up in failure.

Do not waste any more time, money, sweat, determination, and tears trying out another sort of diet. Restricting your food intake while your hormones are not balanced, definitely leaving you with a slow metabolism rate will not make you any slimmer nor healthier.

This is only one of the few things that imbalanced hormones can do to you. There are several others that can affect another aspect of your health without you knowing it.

By now, most likely you already have a vague idea about the hormone reset diet. Think of your body as a plant that is infested and has tons of dead leaves. Cutting just the dead leaves and hoping for a healthy, bright green new leaf sprouting out of it is pointless. The leaves would only grow and wilt quickly, leaving you a new set of dead leaves to get rid of.

It will only become a vicious cycle that doesn't only waste your effort and money. It also wastes your years and health while you are busily figuring out what will work for you.

What I am doing right now is giving you a free pass for the shortcut of figuring out just the right sort of diet for you.

Give yourself a break and address the problem from the root. Sort out the infestation first. At times, it might take longer than usual. Still, at least you now know for yourself that you are doing it correctly.

Not only will it solve your diet problems at hand, it will also help you develop a healthy habit of helping your body optimize your hormones. You may not see the big advantage that it can cause you yet, but as you grow older and your bodily functions start to decrease their productivity, you will find out the importance and impact of what I am teaching you to invest on to.

This guide is not the sort that will only keep you looking good for the summer. It will also make sure that you are feeling good while looking good for the rest of your life.

Breakfast

Broccoli Omelet

Preparation Time: 30 minutes
Cooking Time: 2 hours
Servings: 4
Ingredients:
½ c. milk—2%
6 large eggs
½ t. black pepper
¼ t. of Chili powder
¼ t. of Garlic powder
¼ t. of Salt
1 small onion
3 cloves of garlic
1 c. freshly cut broccoli florets
1 med. chopped tomato
1-2 c. shredded cheddar cheese
¼ c. diced green onion
1 tbsp. parmesan cheese
Shortening/non-stick cooking spray for the pot
Directions:

Grease the slow cooker with the spray/shortening to make clean-up a breeze.

Chop the onion, cut the stems off the broccoli, and mince the garlic. Crack the eggs into a mixing dish, and whisk in the spices and milk. Toss in the minced garlic, onions, florets, and shredded parmesan cheese into the egg mixture.

Cover the cooker and prepare for 1 ½ to 2 hours on the high setting. The edges will brown first. If the pot is cooking too fast, you can switch to the low setting.

Use a sharp knife to cut away the egg from the pot. Remove the darkened portions and sprinkle with the cheese.

Add it to a serving platter and add extra tomatoes, cheese, or other garnishes you desire.

Nutrition:

Calories: 423;

Net Carbs: 10 g;

Fat: 28 g;

Protein: 29 g

Bacon and Shrimp Risotto

Preparation Time: 15 minutes

Cooking Time: 15 minutes

Servings: 2

Ingredients:

Chopped bacon (4 slices)

Daikon/winter radish/ jicama (2 cups)
Dry white wine (2 tbsp.)
Chicken stock (.25 cup)
Garlic clove (1)
Ground pepper (as desired)
Chopped parsley (2 tbsp.)
Cooked shrimp (4 oz.)
Directions:
Cut the skin of the radish and slice. Mince the garlic and chop the bacon. Remove as much water as possible from the daikon once it's shredded.
On the stovetop, warm up a saucepan using the medium heat setting. Toss in the bacon and fry until it's crispy. Leave the drippings in the pan and remove the bacon to drain.
Add the wine, daikon, salt, pepper, stock, and garlic into the pan and cook for six to eight minutes until most of the liquid is absorbed.
Fold in the bacon (save a few bits for the topping) and shrimp along with the parsley.
Serve and enjoy.
Note: If you cannot find the daikon, you can also substitute using some shredded cauliflower in its place.
Nutrition:
Calories: 224;
Protein: 23.7 g;
Fat Content: 9.4 g;
Total Net Carbs: 5.3 g

Sausage & Egg Casserole

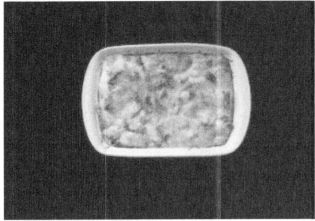

Preparation Time: 30 minutes
Cooking Time: 2 hours - 35 minutes
Servings: 6
Ingredients:
1 med. head of broccoli
1 pkg. low-carb sausage links
1 c. shredded cheddar cheese—divided
10 eggs
¾ c. whipping cream
2 minced garlic cloves
¼ t. pepper
½ t. salt/Suggested: 6-quart slow cooker
Directions:
Chop the broccoli. Mince the garlic and slice the sausage. Grease the pot with some non-stick cooking spray.
Layer the broccoli, sausage, and cheese in two-layer segments (6 layers total).
Combine until well combined, whipping cream, whisked eggs, salt, pepper, and garlic. Add the layered fixings to it.
Secure the lid. Prepare on high for two to three hours or four to five using the low setting. The edges are browned, and the center is set when it is ready to serve.
Nutrition:
Calories: 484;
Net Carbs: 4.21 g;
Fat: 38.9 g;
Protein: 26.13 g

Spinach and Mozzarella Frittata

Preparation Time: 15 minutes
Cooking Time: 1 hour 30 minutes
Servings: 6
Ingredients:
½ c. diced onion
1 tbsp. EVOO
1 c. shredded 2% mozzarella cheese—divided
3 egg whites (+) 3 eggs
2 tbsp. milk—1%
¼ t. of each white & black pepper
1 c. chopped baby spinach—packed
1 diced Roma tomato
To Taste: Salt
Directions:
Cut the stems from the spinach.
Pour the oil into a skillet to sauté the onion (med. heat) for about five minutes. Use a non-stick cooking spray to coat the slow cooker.
Combine ¾ cup of the cheese, the sautéed onion, and the rest of the fixings in a mixing bowl. Add to the pot and sprinkle with the remainder of the cheese.
Secure the lid and cook 1 to 1 ½ hours on low. The eggs will be set.
Test for Doneness: Insert a knife in the center of the pot. If it is clean, they're done.
Nutrition:

Calories: 139;
Net Carbs: 3 g;
Fat: 8 g;
Protein: 12 g

Black Bean Quiche

Preparation Time: 10 minutes
Cooking Time: 10 minutes
Servings: 6
Ingredients:
Eggs (5 whole and 5 whites)
Salt (.5 tsp.)
Water (.33 cup)
Black pepper (.25 tsp.)
Chopped tomato (.5 cup)
Low-sodium black beans (.66 cup)
Grated jack cheese (3 oz.)
For the Garnish: Cilantro
Directions:
Whisk all of the eggs with salt, pepper, and water.
Warm up the oven to 375° Fahrenheit.
Empty the mixture into a greased pie dish coated with a spritz of cooking oil spray.
Sprinkle with the beans, tomatoes, and cheese.

Bake for 30 to 35 minutes until the centers of the eggs are set. Let them cool for about ten minutes and sprinkle using the cilantro before serving.
Nutrition:
Calories: 141.7;
Protein: 10 g;
Fat Content: 8.7 g;
Total Net Carbs: 5.1 g

Tex-Mex Scramble

Preparation Time: 10 minutes
Cooking Time: 15 minutes
Servings: 4
If you like a spicy breakfast, then this is perfect for you. Garnish, if desired, with a little bit of sour cream to cool it down or your favorite guacamole. It cooks quickly, stores well, and reheats easily.
Ingredients:
8 ounces bulk chorizo
6 scallions, both white and green parts, chopped
1 jalapeño pepper, seeded and minced
2 garlic cloves, minced
8 large eggs, beaten
½ cup grated Cheddar cheese
Directions:

In a large nonstick skillet, cook the chorizo over medium-high heat, crumbling with a spatula as you cook, until it is browned, about 5 minutes.

Add the scallions and jalapeño and cook, stirring occasionally, until softened, about 3 minutes more.

Add the garlic and cook, constantly stirring, for 30 seconds.

Add the eggs to the pan.

Cook, scrambling until the eggs are set, about 3 minutes.

Sprinkle with the cheese. Stir once to combine on the heat.

Divide the scramble evenly between 4 storage containers.

Nutrition:

Calories: 508;

Total Fat: 40g;

Saturated Fat: 17g;

Protein: 32g;

Total Carbs: 5g;

Fiber: <1g;

Sugar: 2g;

Sodium: 1,002mg

Broccoli and Tuna

Preparation Time: 5 minutes
Cooking Time: 5 minutes
Servings: 2

Ingredients:
Light tuna (3 oz. can)
Broccoli (1 cup)
Cheese (2 tbsp.)
Salt (1 tsp.)
Directions:
Place the frozen florets of broccoli into a pan of water until they're thawed. Drain.
Mix the broccoli and cheese until melted. Fold in the tuna.
Salt if desired.
Serve any time for a great treat.
Nutrition:
Calories: 122;
Protein: 14.2 g;
Fat Content: 20.6 g;
Total Net Carbs: 3 g

Halloumi Burger

Preparation Time: 15 minutes
Cooking Time: 10 minutes
Servings: 4
Ingredients:
Sour cream (6.7 tbsp.)
Mayonnaise (6.7 tbsp.)

Coconut oil or butter for the pan
Halloumi cheese (15 oz.)
Sliced veggies (your choice)
Directions:
Whisk the mayo and sour cream and cover the bowl. Store in the fridge.
Add the butter to a skillet and add cheese. Cook until lightly browned.
Place on a plate and garnish with the mayo mix and veggies. Serve.
Nutrition:
Calories: 534;
Protein: 23.8 g;
Fat Content: 45.1 g;
Total Net Carbs: 9.4 g

Grilled Chicken with Spinach and Mozzarella

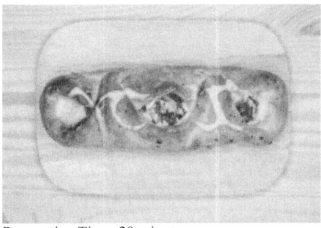

Preparation Time: 20 minutes
Cooking Time: 40 minutes
Servings: 6
Ingredients:
Large chicken breasts (24 oz. or 6 portions)
Olive oil (1 tsp.)
Pepper and Kosher salt (as desired)
Garlic cloves (3 crushed)

Drained frozen spinach (10 oz.)
Roasted red pepper strips packed in water (.5 cup)
Shredded part-skim mozzarella (3 oz.)
Olive oil cooking spray
Directions:
Warm the oven to 400° Fahrenheit.
Prepare the grill/grill pan with the oil.
Sprinkle the salt and pepper onto the chicken. Cook about two to three minutes per side.
Add the oil into a frying pan along with the garlic. Continue cooking for about 30 seconds, add a sprinkle of salt and pepper, and toss in the spinach. Sauté another two to three minutes.
Arrange the chicken on a baking sheet and add the spinach to each one. Top them off with half of the cheese and peppers. Bake for about three minutes until lightly toasted.
Serve.
Nutrition:
Calories: 195;
Protein: 30.9 g;
Fat Content: 6.1 g;
Total Net Carbs: 3.7 g

Lemon Garlic Shrimp Pasta

Preparation Time: 10 minutes

Cooking Time: 15 minutes
Servings: 4
Ingredients:
Angel hair pasta (2 bags)
Garlic cloves (4)
Olive oil (2 tbsp.)
Butter (2 tbsp.)
Lemon (.5 of 1)
Large raw shrimp (1 lb.)
Paprika (.5 tsp.)
Fresh basil (as desired)
Pepper and salt (as desired)
Directions:
Drain the water from the package of noodles and rinse them in cold water. Add them to a pot of boiling water for two minutes. Transfer to a hot skillet over medium heat to remove the excess liquid (dry roast). Set them aside.
Use the same pan to warm the butter, oil, and mashed garlic. Sauté for a few minutes, but don't brown.
Slice the lemon into rounds and add them to the garlic along with the shrimp. Sauté for approximately three minutes per side.
Add the noodles and spices and stir to blend the flavors.
Nutrition:
Calories: 360;
Protein: 36 g;
Fat Content: 21 g;
Total Net Carbs: 3.5 g

Divine Breakfast Casserole

Preparation Time: 20 minutes
Cooking Time: 1 hour 30 minutes
Servings: 4
Ingredients:
6 large eggs
3 large bacon slices
3 tbsp. shallots
1 c. chopped white mushrooms
½ c. chopped red bell pepper

8 large kale leaves
To Taste: Salt & pepper
1 c. shredded parmesan cheese/your favorite
Optional:
Sliced avocado
Spinach
EVOO (oil)
Directions:
Prepare the bacon by cooking it in a skillet until it's crispy. Finely shred the kale leaves and chop the stems into small chunks.
Toss in the shallot, mushroom, and red pepper with the cooked bacon. Sauté until softened. Blend in the kale and turn off the heat to the skillet.
Whisk the eggs, salt, and pepper until mixed well.
Program the slow cooker on the high setting to warm up and add the butter. Once it melts, use a brush to swirl the butter around the pot to help prevent it from sticking.
Add the sautéed veggies to the slow cooker and sprinkle with the cheese. Dump the egg mixture into the cooker and set the timer for 1 ½ hrs. On the high setting or six on the low.
Garnish as you choose. You can enjoy it for two days if stored in the fridge.
Nutrition:
Calories: 313;
Net Carbs: 4.0 g;
Fat: 22.2 g;
Protein: 22.9 g

Egg Bacon & Cheese Casserole

Preparation Time: 30 minutes
Cooking Time: 2 hours
Servings: 6
Ingredients:
8 slices thick-cut bacon
1 bag (20 oz.) hash browns—frozen shredded
1 pkg. (8 oz.) shredded cheddar cheese
6 thinly sliced green onions
¼ t. pepper

½ t. salt
12 eggs
½ c. milk
For the Slow Cooker: Oil/cooking spray
Directions:
Prepare the bacon. Cook and coarsely chop the bacon.
Lightly grease the cooker.
Layer the hash browns with approximately ½ of the bacon, and ½ of the cheese, and 1/3 of the onions. (Reserve some of the onion and bacon for the garnishes.) Make a second layer using the rest of the hash browns, bacon, cheese, and onions.
Whisk the eggs, salt, pepper, and milk, and dump over the layers.
Cook for approximately four to five hours on low. You may also speed it up on the high setting for two to three hours.
When ready to serve, add the reserved bacon and onions.
Nutrition:
Calories: 342;
Net Carbs: 14 g;
Protein: 21 g;
Fat: 22 g

Overnight Oats

Preparation Time: 5 minutes
Cooking Time: 1 hour to overnight
Servings: 2
Ingredients:
1/3 c. of each:
Unsweetened almond milk
Hemp hearts
2 t. chia seeds
2 tbsp. almond butter
Directions:
Measure all the ingredients in two glass jars.
Refrigerate overnight or a minimum of one hour.
Enjoy a healthy breakfast on-the-run.
Nutrition:
Net Carbs: 7 g;
Fat: 22 g;

Protein: 13 g

Coconut Flour Pancakes

Preparation Time: 10 minutes
Cooking Time: 15 minutes
Servings: 6
Coconut flour has a great texture for pancakes, and these don't taste super coconutty. While you may be tempted to make the batter ahead and cook the pancakes fresh, I don't recommend it. Cook these pancakes before you store them. As time passes, coconut flour soaks up more and more liquid, making the batter difficult to work with if it sits. Top with a sugar-free, low-carb pancake syrup or with a few berries and whipped cream sweetened with a pinch of erythritol.
Ingredients:
1 cup melted unsalted butter or coconut oil
1 cup heavy (whipping) cream or full-fat coconut milk
8 large eggs, beaten
1 teaspoon vanilla extract
1 cup coconut flour
1 tablespoon erythritol
2 teaspoons baking soda
Pinch salt
Directions:
In a medium bowl, whisk together the butter, cream, eggs, and vanilla.
In a large bowl, whisk together the coconut flour, erythritol, baking soda, and salt.
Add the wet ingredients to the dry and mix until just combined.
Heat a nonstick griddle or skillet over medium-high. Brush with a little melted butter or coconut oil.
In ¼-cup portions, spoon the batter onto the hot griddle. Cook until bubbles form on top, about 2 minutes.
Flip with a spatula. Cook 2 to 3 minutes more, or until lightly browned on the bottom.
Into each of 6 storage containers, place 3 pancakes.
Nutrition:
Calories: 518;
Total Fat: 40g;

Protein: 13g;
Total Carbs: 31g;
Fiber: 16g;
Net Carbs: 15g;
Sodium: 646mg

Omelet-Stuffed Baked Bell Peppers

Preparation Time: 10 minutes
Cooking Time: 55 minutes
Servings: 4
These peppers make a perfect breakfast on the go because they store well and reheat in the microwave. Use any color bell pepper you like. Be sure to remove any seeds or fibrous ribs from the peppers to help reduce bitterness and heat.
Ingredients:
2 Red bell peppers, halved lengthwise, seeds and ribs removed
½ pound bulk Italian sausage
4 Ounces mushrooms, sliced
8 large eggs, beaten
¼ cup heavy (whipping) cream
1 teaspoon Italian seasoning
1/2 teaspoon salt
1/8 teaspoon freshly ground black pepper
Pinch red pepper flakes
½ cup grated Parmesan cheese
Directions:
Preheat the oven to 400 Fahrenheit.
Place the peppers on a rimmed baking sheet with the cut sides up. Bake in the oven for 5 minutes to soften.
Meanwhile, in a large nonstick skillet, heat the sausage over medium-high heat, crumbling with a spoon, until it is browned, about 5 minutes.
Add the mushrooms and cook, stirring occasionally, until soft, another 5 minutes. Cool slightly.
In a bowl, whisk together the eggs, cream, Italian seasoning, and salt, pepper, and red pepper flakes.
Fold in the cooled sausage and mushrooms.
Pour the mixture into the pepper halves. Sprinkle with the cheese.

Return to the oven. Cook until the eggs are set, and the cheese is browned, about 40 minutes. Let cool.

Into each of 4 storage containers, place 1 stuffed pepper half.

Substitution Tip: Replace the Italian sausage with ½ pound of bacon or pancetta, fried and crumbled.

Nutrition:

Calories: 459;

Total Fat: 34g;

Protein: 33g;

Total Carbs: 7g;

Net Carbs: 6g;

Fiber: 1g;

Sodium: 1,048mg

Bacon-Asparagus Breakfast Muffins

Preparation Time: 10 minutes

Cooking Time: 25 minutes

Servings: 6

If you only have a 6-cup muffin tin, then you can halve this recipe. Silicone muffin tins are especially good for making breakfast egg muffins because they release so easily. Feel free to vary the ham or veggies in this recipe.

Ingredients:

Coconut oil, butter, or extra-virgin olive oil for greasing

4 tablespoons (½ stick) unsalted butter

8 Ounces bacon, chopped

½ onion, chopped

1 pound asparagus, trimmed and cut into bite-size pieces

1 cup shredded Gruyère or Swiss cheese

10 large eggs, beaten

¼ cup heavy (whipping) cream

1 teaspoon Dijon mustard

1 teaspoon dried rosemary

1/2 teaspoon salt

1/8 teaspoon freshly ground black pepper

Directions:

Preheat the oven to 375°F. Grease a 12-cup muffin tin.

In a large nonstick skillet, heat the butter over medium-high until it bubbles. Add the bacon and cook until it browns, about 5 minutes. Add the onion and asparagus and cook, stirring occasionally, until the vegetables are tender, about 5 minutes.

Spoon into the prepared muffin cups.

Sprinkle with the cheese.

In a large bowl, whisk together the eggs, cream, mustard, rosemary, salt, and pepper.

Pour over the vegetables and cheese in the muffin cups.

Bake in the preheated oven until the eggs are set, 12 to 15 minutes.

Let cool slightly and remove the muffins from the tin. Into each of 6 storage containers, place 2 muffins.

Nutrition:

Calories: 411;

Total Fat: 31g;

Protein: 27g;

Total Carbs: 7g;

Net Carbs: 5g;

Fiber: 2g;

Sodium: 900mg

Beef and Cheddar Platter

Preparation Time: 10 minutes

Cooking Time: 10 minutes

Servings: 5

Ingredients:

Deli roast beef (7 oz.)

Cheddar cheese (5 oz.)

Avocado (1)

Radishes (6)

Scallion (1)

Mayonnaise (.5 cup)

Dijon mustard (1 tbsp.)

Lettuce (2 oz.)

Olive oil (2 tbsp.)

Salt and pepper (to your liking)

Directions:

Slice the onion.

Place the cheese, roast beef, radishes, and avocado on a serving platter.
Add the sliced onion, a dollop of mayo, and mustard.
Serve with lettuce and a spritz of olive oil.
Nutrition:
Calories: 1072;
Protein: 38 g;
Fat Content: 98 g;
Total Net Carbs: 6 g

Cauliflower and Mushroom Risotto

Preparation Time: 10 minutes
Cooking Time: 5 minutes
Servings: 4
Ingredients:
Grated head of cauliflower (1)
Vegetable stock (1 cup)
Chopped mushrooms (9 oz.)
Butter (2 tbsp.)
Coconut cream (1 cup)
Pepper and Salt (to taste)
Directions:
Pour the stock into a saucepan. Boil and set aside.
Prepare a skillet with butter. Sauté the mushrooms until golden.
Grate and stir in the cauliflower and stock.
Simmer and add the cream, cooking until the cauliflower is al dente.
Serve.
Nutrition:
Calories: 186;
Protein: 1 g;
Fat Content: 17.1 g;
Total Net Carbs: 4.3 g

Chicken Sausage Corn Dogs

Preparation Time: 5 minutes

Cooking Time: 5 minutes
Servings: 4
Ingredients:
Chicken sausage (4 links)
Lard (1.5 cups)
Almond flour (1 cup)
Ms. Dash Table Blend (1 tsp.)
Kosher salt (.5 tsp.)
Baking powder (1 tsp.)
Turmeric (.5 tsp.)
Cayenne pepper (.25 tsp.)
Large eggs (2)
Heavy whipping cream (2 tbsp.)
For the Pan: Oil (1.5 cups)
Directions:
Combine the spices and almond meal.
In another dish, whisk the heavy cream, egg, and add the baking powder to the mixture.
Heat a saucepan with the oil (400° Fahrenheit approximately).
Dip the dogs/sausages into the mixture and add them to the oil. Fry for approximately two minutes for each side.
Transfer to a plate of paper towels to drain. Serve.
Nutrition:
Calories: 494;
Protein: 15.4 g;
Fat Content: 45.9 g;
Total Net Carbs: 4.5 g

Grilled Buffalo Chicken Lettuce Wraps

Preparation Time: 15 minutes
Cooking Time: 40 minutes
Servings: 15
Ingredients:
Franks Red Hot Sauce (.75 cup)
Boneless and skinless breasts of chicken (3 large)
Lettuce cups (15)
Avocado (1 diced)
Cherry tomatoes (.75 cup)

Ranch dressing (.5 cup)
Sliced green onions (.25 cup)
Also Needed: Grill basket or kabob sticks
Directions:
Dice up the chicken into ½- inch cubes. Slice the tomatoes into halves. Set aside for now.
Place the chicken in a dish and add Frank's sauce (or your choice). Put a lid or foil over the container and put it in the refrigerator for about 30 minutes.
Set the grill temperature to 400° Fahrenheit.
Arrange the grill basket with the chicken/kabobs on the grill and cook for 8-10 minutes. Stir constantly. Take them from the grill and dump them into a container with the remainder of the buffalo sauce.
Prepare the lettuce cups with two to three cubes of chicken, two to three diced tomatoes, a pinch of onions, two to three diced avocados, and a drizzle of dressing.
Nutrition:
Calories: 53;
Protein: 5 g;
Fat Content: 3 g;
Total Net Carbs: 2 g

Mains

Chunky Chili Wrap

Preparation Time: 20 minutes
Cooking Time: 8 hours
Servings: 4
Ingredients:
1 pound lean ground beef
1 carrot, peeled, diced
1 medium onion, diced
1 celery stalk, diced
2 tomatoes, diced
1/2 cup water
4 cloves garlic, minced
1 tsp. oregano, cumin, paprika
1 tsp. salt, coarse black pepper
Extra virgin olive oil
4 flax tortillas
Directions:
Lightly coat 4 qt. slow cooker with olive oil.
Place all ingredients in slow cooker and cook on low overnight for eight hours.
In the morning, spoon chilli into tortillas, roll and enjoy.
Nutrition:
Calories 242
Carbs 10
Fat 13
Protein 30
Sodium 141

Bacon Bite Wraps

Preparation Time: 10 minutes
Cooking Time: 10 minutes

Servings: 4
Ingredients:
8 slices bacon
2 cucumbers
4 eggs, hard boiled
1/2 tsp. salt, black pepper
Directions:
Peel eggs and mix in food processor until fairly smooth.
Heat skillet and cook bacon slices for three minutes per side.
Using mandolin, slice cucumbers into long pliable strips.
Place one slice cucumber on flat surface, half slice of bacon, dollop of egg and roll like sushi.
Repeat with remaining ingredients.
Nutrition:
Calories 292
Carbs 6
Fat 20
Protein 21
Sodium 942

Creamy Avocado Egg Salad Wrap

Preparation Time: 10 minutes
Cooking Time: 10 minutes
Servings: 4
Ingredients:
4 eggs, hard boiled
1 red bell pepper, seeded and chopped
1 celery stalk, chopped
1/2 avocado
1 lemon, juiced
1/2 tsp. salt, black pepper
4 almond wraps
Directions:
Peel eggs, chop and mix with celery, bell pepper in glass bowl.
Place avocado in blender and mix until smooth, add lemon juice, salt, pepper.
Add avocado to bowl and mix.
Place a quarter of mixture in each wrap.

Nutrition:
Calories 124
Carbs 4
Fat 9
Protein 6
Sodium 68

Cashew Butter and Banana Wrap

Preparation Time: 10 minutes
Cooking Time: 10 minutes
Servings: 4
Ingredients:
1 cup cashews, soaked overnight
3 tbsp. sesame oil
¼ tsp. salt
2 bananas, peeled and sliced
4 flax wraps
Directions:
Place cashews, sesame oil, salt in food processor and mix, scrape sides of bowl intermittently to ensure smooth mixture.
Spread each wrap with cashew butter, add banana and wrap it up for breakfast.
Nutrition:
Calories 339
Carbs 24
Fat 26
Protein 6
Sodium 153

Smoked Salmon and Eggs Wrap

Preparation Time: 10 minutes
Cooking Time: 10 minutes
Servings: 4
Ingredients:
4 slices smoked salmon

6 eggs
¼ cup radish, shredded
1 lemon, juiced
½ tsp. salt, pepper
4 almond wraps
Directions:
Mix radish with lemon juice, set aside.
Whisk eggs with salt, pepper.
Heat 2 tbsp. extra virgin olive oil in nonstick pan.
Pour eggs into pan and cook a minute per side.
Divide omelette into four sections.
Place a quarter of omelette on almond wrap, top with smoked salmon and shredded radish and roll.
Nutrition:
Calories 217
Carbs 6
Fat 7
Protein 27
Sodium 269

Gourmet Chicken Caesar Wrap

Preparation Time: 15 minutes
Cooking Time: 20 minutes
Servings: 4
Ingredients:
1 lb. chicken breasts
3 tbsp. sardines, chopped
1 egg
1 tsp. dry mustard
½ lemon, juiced
2 cups green leaf lettuce, chopped
½ tsp. salt, black pepper
Extra virgin olive oil
Directions:
Preheat oven to 375 degrees and lightly coat glass baking dish with olive oil.
Combine sardines, egg, dry mustard, lemon juice, salt and pepper in food processor and mix until creamy.

Place chicken breasts in bottom of glass baking dish and pour creamy sauce over top.
Bake in oven for 20 minutes turning halfway.
Slice chicken breasts into strips, place on wrap alongside lettuce and wrap.
Nutrition:
Calories 246
Carbs 0
Fat 10
Protein 35
Sodium 148

Sweet Potato Burrito with Caramelized Onions

Preparation Time: 15 minutes
Cooking Time: 25 minutes
Servings: 4
Ingredients:
2 sweet potatoes
1 large onion, sliced
1 red bell pepper, seeded and sliced
1/2 cup cashew, soaked overnight, crushed
1 tsp. dry mustard
2 tbsp. lemon juice
1/2 tsp. cayenne, oregano, cumin
1 tsp. salt, black pepper
Extra virgin olive oil
4 flax tortillas
Directions:
Peel sweet potato, chop and place in steamer for 20 minutes or until soft.
Heat 2 tbsp. olive oil in skillet and sauté onion and bell pepper, add cashew and sauté for a minute, set aside.
Mash sweet potato and mix with spices.
Spoon a quarter of potato mixture into each wrap, top with sautéed onion, bell pepper and cashew, and roll into burrito.
Nutrition:
Calories 345
Carbs 63

Fat 8
Protein 6
Sodium 21

Chicken Cabbage Wraps

Preparation Time: 10 minutes
Cooking Time: 10 minutes
Servings: 4
Ingredients:
1 lb. chicken breasts, roasted
1 red bell pepper, seeded, chopped
1 celery stalk, finely chopped
1 onion, peeled and chopped
4 cloves garlic
1 lemon, juiced
1/2 head cabbage
1 tsp. salt, pepper
Directions:
Heat large pot of water until boiling.
Separate cabbage leaves and place in boiling water for two minutes, remove and run under cold water.
Chop chicken breasts into ½" pieces, place in large bowl and mix with remaining ingredients save cabbage.
Spoon chicken mixture into cabbage leaves and secure roll with toothpick or enjoy open faced.
Nutrition:
Calories 246
Carbs 0
Fat 10
Protein 35
Sodium 148

Sausage and Pepper Wrap

Preparation Time: 10 minutes
Cooking Time: 15 minutes

Servings: 4
Ingredients:
2 lean Italian sausage links
1 onion, sliced
2 red bell peppers
1 green bell pepper
4 cloves, garlic, minced
Salt and pepper to taste
Extra virgin olive oil
4 flax tortillas
Directions:
Slice sausage into ½" rounds.
Heat 2 tbsp. olive oil in skillet, add sausage, sauté.
Add bell peppers, onion, and garlic and continue to sauté until onion is golden brown.
Spoon sausage and peppers into flax tortilla.
Nutrition:
Calories 180
Carbs 14
Fat 5
Protein 20
Sodium 640

Tropical Mango Chicken

Preparation Time: 10 minutes
Cooking Time: 10 minutes
Servings: 4
Ingredients:
1 lb. chicken breasts
1/2 cup mango, chopped
1/4 cup parsley, chopped
2 tbsp. coconut cream
1 tsp. paprika
1 tsp. salt, black pepper
Extra virgin olive oil
4 almond wraps
Directions:
Combine mango, parsley, coconut cream in bowl, set aside.

Slice chicken breast into strips.

Heat 2 tbsp. olive oil in skillet, add chicken breast and sauté until golden brown.

Sprinkle with paprika, salt, pepper and spoon into wraps.

Top with mango chutney and roll them up.

Nutrition:

Calories 321

Carbs 19

Fat 14

Protein 35

Sodium 148

Fall Apple Bacon Chicken Wrap

Preparation Time: 15 minutes

Cooking Time: 8 hours

Servings: 4

Ingredients:

4 slices bacon

3/4 lb. chicken breast, skinless, boneless

2 Granny Smith Apples, peeled, chopped

1 lemon, juiced

1/2 tsp. thyme

1 tsp. salt, black pepper

Extra virgin olive oil

4 flax tortillas

Directions:

Coat 4 qt. slow cooker with olive oil.

Place apples in bottom of pot, top with chicken, bacon and spices.

Cook on low overnight for 8 hours.

Nutrition:

Calories 318

Carbs 23

Fat 21

Protein 35

Sodium 843

Tomato Zucchini Wrap

Preparation Time: 10 minutes
Cooking Time: 20 minutes
Servings: 4
Ingredients:
2 tomatoes, chopped
1 cup basil, chopped
6 garlic cloves, minced
1 onion, chopped
4 zucchinis
1 tsp. oregano
1 tsp. salt, black pepper
Directions:
Preheat oven to 375 degrees and coat baking tray with olive oil.
Slice off ends of zucchini and using mandolin slice long strips, set aside.
Heat olive oil in skillet and sauté onion, garlic for a minute.
In a bowl combine garlic mixture with tomato, basil, oregano, salt, black pepper.
Place two strips zucchini on flat surface, spoon, tomato basil inside, roll up and secure with toothpick.
Repeat with remaining ingredients and place in baking tray.
Bake for 20 minutes.
Nutrition:
Calories 117
Carbs 12
Fat 7
Protein 3
Sodium 22

Salmon, Cherry and Arugula Flax Seed Wrap

Preparation Time: 10 minutes
Cooking Time: 10 minutes
Servings: 2
Ingredients:
6 oz. salmon, shredded

1 cup arugula
1 lemon, juiced
1/4 cup cherries, pitted, halved
1/4 tsp. salt
1/2 tsp. coarse black pepper
2 flaxseed tortillas
Directions:
Toss together salmon, cherries, salt and pepper.
Spoon half of salmon filling into each flax wrap, top with half cup of arugula and roll.
Nutrition:
Calories 144
Carbs 7
Fat 5
Protein 17
Sodium 45

Meatballs with Fresh Mint Sauce Wrap

Preparation Time: 20 minutes
Cooking Time: 20 minutes
Servings: 4
Ingredients:
Meatballs
1 lb. lean ground beef
5 cloves garlic, peeled, minced
2 tbsp. tomato puree
1 egg
1/2 tsp. cumin
1 tsp. each salt, pepper
Mint Sauce
3 cups mint, stemmed, chopped
1 lemon, juiced
1/4 cup extra virgin olive oil
1/2 tsp. salt
1/2 tsp. cayenne
Wrap
4 almond wraps
1 onion, sliced

Directions:

Preheat oven to 400 degrees and coat baking tray with extra virgin olive oil.

For meatballs, whisk egg in bowl, add remaining ingredients, and combine well.

Roll 2" meatballs, place on baking tray and bake for 20 minutes.

For mint chutney, place ingredients in blender and mix until well combined.

Place three meatballs on wrap, top with chutney and some fresh onion.

Nutrition:

Calories 235

Carbs 2

Fat 8

Protein 36

Sodium 93

Hummus Wrap

Preparation Time: 10 minutes

Cooking Time: 10 minutes

Servings: 4

Ingredients:

Filling

3 cups roasted turkey, shredded

¼ cup walnuts, crushed

1 tsp. paprika

1 lemon, juiced

1 tsp. salt, black pepper

Paleo Hummus

4 cups cauliflower florets

1 tbsp. organic tahini

4 cloves garlic, minced

2 tbsp. extra virgin olive oil

4 cauliflower wraps

Directions:

Place ingredients for Paleo Hummus in food processor and mix until semi-smooth.

Heat skillet and cook hummus for three minutes, set aside.

Mix turkey, walnuts, paprika, lemon, salt and pepper.
Spread hummus on cauliflower wraps, spoon filling on tortilla and wrap.
Nutrition:
Calories 149
Carbs 1
Fat 6
Protein 23
Sodium 671

Tex-Mex Wrap Explosion

Preparation Time: 10 minutes
Cooking Time: 15 minutes
Servings: 4
Ingredients:
1 lb. sirloin steak
4 cloves garlic, minced
2 onions, sliced
1 green bell pepper, seeded and sliced
1 lime, juiced
1 tsp. cayenne
1 tsp. each salt, pepper
Extra virgin olive oil
4 flax wraps
Directions:
Slice sirloin steak into strips, set aside
Heat 2 tbsp. olive oil in skillet, add steak and stir-fry until browned.
Remove steak into bowl, set aside.
Add onion, bell pepper to skillet, sauté for two minutes.
Return steak into skillet, add spices, sauté for a minute.
Turn off heat, cover and allow to rest for 10 minutes.
Spoon ¼ of beef sauté into each wrap and drizzle with a little lime juice.
Nutrition:
Calories 248
Carbs 8
Fat 7
Protein 35

Sodium 76

Pomegranate Chicken in Lettuce Wraps

Preparation Time: 15 minutes
Cooking Time: 15 minutes
Servings: 4
Ingredients:
1 lb. Chicken breast
1/2 cup pomegranate seeds
1 lemon juiced
1/4 cup walnuts, chopped
8 large Romaine lettuce leaves
Extra virgin olive oil
Directions:
Slice chicken breast into thin strips.
Place 2 tbsp. olive oil in skillet and sauté chicken until golden brown.
Add nuts and pomegranate seeds, sauté for two minutes.
Squeeze lemon juice on top, cover and allow to cool.
Lay down two pieces romaine lettuce and spoon chicken pomegranate chicken into leaves and roll into wrap.
Nutrition:
Calories 347
Carbs 14
Fat 23
Protein 39
Sodium 145

Paleo Pesto Chicken Wrap

Preparation Time: 15 minutes
Cooking Time: 30 minutes
Servings: 4
Ingredients:
1 lb. chicken breasts, boneless, skinless
1 onion, diced

8 cloves garlic,
1 cup fresh basil
¼ cup pine nuts
½ cup cashews, soaked overnight
½ cup water
1 tsp. salt, pepper
Extra virgin olive oil
4 cauliflower wraps
Directions:
Preheat oven to 375 degrees and coat baking dish with olive oil.
Place basil, garlic, pine nuts, cashews, salt, pepper, water and ¼ cup olive oil in food processor and mix until smooth, set aside.
Place chicken in baking dish and coat with ¾ of basil mixture, bake in oven for 30 minutes turning halfway.
Slice chicken into strips, place on wraps and spoon a little remaining basil mixture in each wrap.
Nutrition:
Calories 393
Carbs 11
Fat 22
Protein 37
Sodium 102

Stuffed Italian Wrap

Preparation Time: 10 minutes
Cooking Time: 10 minutes
Servings: 4
Ingredients:
1 lb. lean ground beef
2 cups tomato puree
4 cups cauliflower florets
1 onion, diced
4 cloves garlic, minced
1 tsp. oregano
4 cloves, ground
1 basil leaf
1 tsp. salt, black pepper
Extra virgin olive oil

4 almond wraps
Directions:
Place cauliflower florets in food processor and puree until rice-like granules form.
Heat 2 tbsp. olive oil in skillet, add onion, garlic and sauté for a minute.
Add beef and brown.
Add tomato, cloves, salt, and pepper, turn heat to low and simmer for 10 minutes.
Add cauliflower, simmer for another five minutes.
Remove basil leaf, spoon mixture into wraps and roll tightly.
Nutrition:
Calories 299
Carbs 20
Fat 7
Protein 39
Sodium 140

Pork and Sweet Potato Comfort Wrap

Preparation Time: 10 minutes
Cooking Time: 10 minutes
Servings: 4
Ingredients:
1 lb. pork chops, boneless
1 sweet potato, peeled and cubed
1 onion, diced
1 tsp. fresh rosemary
1 tsp. salt, black pepper
Extra virgin olive oil
4 almond wraps
Directions:
Steam sweet potato for 20 minutes.
Slice pork chops into strips.
In skillet, heat 2 tbsp. olive oil, sauté onion, garlic for a minute, add pork strips, and continue sauté for another five minutes.
Cover, reduce heat and allow to sit for 10 minutes.
Mash sweet potato with ghee, rosemary, salt, pepper.
Spoon sweet potato into wrap and top with pork strips.

Nutrition:
Calories 466
Carbs 24
Fat 28
Protein 28
Sodium 116

Chicken & Poultry Recipes

Honey & Orange Chicken

Preparation Time: 30 minutes
Cooking Time: 4 hours
Servings: 6
Ingredients:
1/4 cup honey
3 tablespoons low sodium soy sauce
2 tablespoons orange juice
2 teaspoons orange zest
1-1/2 tablespoons ginger, minced
3 cloves garlic, minced
1/4 teaspoon red pepper, crushed
1 tablespoon rice vinegar
Cooking spray
12 chicken drumsticks (skinless)
Directions:
In a bowl, mix the honey, soy sauce, orange juice, orange zest, ginger, garlic, red pepper and vinegar.
Coat the slow cooker with the cooking spray.
Add the chicken to the slow cooker.
Pour in the honey mixture.
Toss to coat.
Cover the pot.
Cook on low for 4 hours.
Transfer some of the liquid to a skillet over medium heat.
Bring to a boil and then simmer until reduced to half.
Pour the sauce over the chicken before serving.
Serving Suggestion:
Sprinkle top with toasted sesame seeds and serve with fresh cilantro.
Tip:
Use freshly squeezed orange juice.
Nutrition:
Calories252

Fat 7g
Saturated Fat 2g
Fiber 0g
Carbohydrates 18g
Protein 29g
Cholesterol 150mg
Sugars 16g
Sodium 416 mg
Potassium 352 mg

Greek Chicken with Veggies

Preparation Time: 30 minutes
Cooking Time: 4 hours and 15 minutes
Servings: 6
Ingredients:
1 lb. potatoes, sliced into cubes
1 lb. carrots, sliced into cubes
2 lb. chicken thighs (boneless, skinless)
1/4 cup dry white wine
14 oz. low sodium chicken broth
4 cloves garlic, minced
Salt and pepper to taste
15 oz. artichoke hearts, rinsed and sliced into wedges
1 egg
2 egg yolks
1/4 cup lemon juice
1/4 cup fresh dill, chopped
Directions:
Arrange the potatoes and carrots on the bottom of the slow cooker.
Place the chicken on top of the vegetables.
In a skillet over medium high heat, pour the wine, broth, garlic and salt.
Bring to a boil then simmer.
Pour the sauce over the chicken and veggies.
Cover the pot.
Cook on low for 4 hours.
Add the artichokes and cook on high for 5 minutes.
In a bowl, whisk the egg, egg yolks and lemon juice.

Add 1/2 cup of the cooking liquid into the eggs.
Mix well.
Cover for 15 minutes.
Add the dill and pepper.
Drizzle the sauce over the chicken and veggies before serving.
Serving Suggestion:
Serve with fresh green salad.
Tip:
Use freshly squeezed lemon juice.
Nutrition:
Calories326
Fat 10g
Saturated Fat 3g
Fiber 5g
Carbohydrates 28g
Protein 29g
Cholesterol 214mg
Sugars 5g
Sodium 778mg
Potassium 822mg

Chicken with Mushroom & Herbs

Preparation Time: 30 minutes
Cooking Time: 7 hours
Servings: 4
Ingredients:
1-1/2 cups frozen whole onions
8 oz. button mushrooms, sliced in half
1/4 cup dry red wine
1/2 cup low sodium chicken broth
2 tablespoons tomato paste
1/2 teaspoon dried thyme
1/2 teaspoon dried rosemary
1/2 teaspoon garlic salt
Pepper to taste
1 bay leaf
8 chicken thighs, skin removed
2 tablespoons whole wheat flour

1/4 cup low sodium chicken stock
Directions:
In a slow cooker, add the onions and mushrooms.
Pour in the wine, broth and tomato paste.
Season with the thyme, rosemary, garlic salt and pepper.
Add the bay leaf. Mix well.
Place the chicken inside the cooker and coat with the mixture.
Cover the pot.
Cook on low for 7 hours.
Transfer the chicken and vegetables on a serving platter.
Remove the bay leaf.
Cover with foil.
Remove the fat from the cooking liquid.
Add 2 cups of the cooking liquid to a pan over medium heat.
In a bowl, mix the flour and chicken stock.
Pour this into the pan.
Cook until the sauce has thickened.
Pour the sauce over the chicken and vegetables.
Serving Suggestion:
Serve with mashed potatoes.
Tip:
You can also cook this dish on high for 4 hours.
Nutrition:
Calories215
Fat 5g
Saturated Fat 1g
Fiber 2g
Carbohydrates 10g
Protein 29g
Cholesterol 107mg
Sugars 4g
Sodium 342mg
Potassium 515mg

Cajun Chicken & Shrimp

Preparation Time: 30 minutes
Cooking Time: 5 hours
Servings: 8

Ingredients:
1/4 teaspoon paprika
1/4 teaspoon garlic powder
1/4 teaspoon onion powder
1/4 teaspoon black pepper
1/4 teaspoon white pepper
1/8 teaspoon cayenne pepper
1 lb. chicken breast (boneless and skinless), sliced into cubes
2 onions, chopped
2 cloves garlic, minced
4 stalks celery, sliced thinly
14-1/2 oz. low sodium chicken broth
6 oz. unsalted tomato paste
15 oz. tomatoes, diced
Salt to taste
1-1/2 cups uncooked brown rice
3/4 cup sweet pepper, chopped
8 oz. cooked shrimp, cooked and deveined
1/4 cup fresh parsley, chopped
Directions:
In a bowl, combine the paprika, garlic powder, onion powder, black and white pepper, and cayenne pepper.
In a slow cooker, add the chicken, onion, garlic, celery, broth, tomato paste, diced tomatoes and salt.
Sprinkle the paprika mixture all over the chicken and vegetables.
Mix well.
Seal the pot.
Cook on low for 4 ½ hours.
Add the rice and sweet peppers.
Mix well.
Cover the pot.
Cook for 30 minutes or until rice is fully cooked.
Add in the shrimp and parsley.
Serving Suggestion:
Garnish with fresh celery leaves.
Tip:
You don't need to remove the shrimp tails.
Nutrition:
Calories211
Fat 2g

Saturated Fat 2g
Fiber 4g
Carbohydrates 26g
Protein 23g
Cholesterol 88mg
Sugars 6g
Sodium 415mg
Potassium 340mg

Spicy Barbecue Chicken

Preparation Time: 15 minutes
Cooking Time: 6 hours
Servings: 4
Ingredients:
1/2 cup tomato sauce
2 tablespoons lemon juice
2 tablespoons jalapeño pepper jelly
1/4 teaspoon red pepper, crushed
1 teaspoon brown sugar
2 tablespoons quick-cooking tapioca
1 teaspoon ground cumin
8 chicken drumsticks, skin removed
Directions:
Put all the ingredients in the slow cooker.
Toss to coat evenly.
Seal the pot.
Cook on low for 6 hours.
Serving Suggestion:
Serve with whole grain bread slices.
Tip:
Use half teaspoon red pepper if you like it spicier.
Nutrition:
Calories166
Fat 2g
Saturated Fat 2g
Fiber 4g
Carbohydrates 26g
Protein 23g

Cholesterol 88mg
Sugars 6g
Sodium 415mg
Potassium 340mg

Creamy Turkey

Preparation Time: 30 minutes
Cooking Time: 4 hours
Servings: 6
Ingredients:
2 teaspoons olive oil
1/2 cup shallots, chopped
1 lb. mushrooms, stems trimmed
1/2 cup water, divided
1 cup carrots, sliced thinly
4 cups low sodium chicken broth
2 bay leaves
1 teaspoon fresh thyme leaves
2 lb. turkey (boneless, skinless), sliced into cubes
1/2 teaspoon lemon zest
2 lemon slices with peel, seeded
2 tablespoons corn starch
1/4 cup whipping cream
2 tablespoons lemon juice
Salt and pepper to taste
1-1/2 cups frozen green peas, rinsed
1/2 cup parsley, chopped
Directions:
Pour the olive oil in a skillet over high heat.
Add the shallots and mushrooms.
Pour in half of the water.
Cover the skillet, and cook for 4 minutes, stirring occasionally.
Uncover and cook for 10 minutes.
Add the carrots, broth, bay leaves and thyme.
Bring to a boil.
Put the turkey inside the slow cooker.
Place the lemon slices on top.
Pour the mushroom mixture over the turkey and lemon.

Cover and cook on high for 3 hours and 30 minutes.
Transfer the turkey and vegetables into a bowl.
Remove the lemon slices and bay leaves.
Pour the cooking liquid into a skillet.
Remove the fat.
Add the lemon zest.
Bring to a boil.
Simmer until reduced.
Mix corn starch and water in a bowl.
Add this and the cream to the pan.
Cook until the sauce has thickened.
Season with the salt and pepper.
Add the peas and parsley before serving.
Serving Suggestion:
This goes well with a bowl of egg noodles.
Tip:
Use freshly grated lemon zest.
Nutrition:
Calories319
Fat 15g
Saturated Fat 5g
Fiber 3g
Carbohydrates 16g
Protein 31g
Cholesterol 99mg
Sugars 5g
Sodium 701mg
Potassium 857mg

Turkey Parmesan Meatballs

Preparation Time: 30 minutes
Cooking Time: 3 hours
Servings: 10
Ingredients:
1 onion, grated
2 cloves garlic, minced
28 oz. tomatoes, chopped
1/4 cup dry red wine

1/2 teaspoon dried oregano
1/2 teaspoon dried basil
Salt and pepper to taste
1 lb. ground turkey
1 egg, beaten
1/2 teaspoon garlic powder
1/2 cup whole wheat breadcrumbs
1/2 cup Parmesan cheese, grated
30 mozzarella balls
Directions:
Put the onion, garlic, tomatoes, red wine, oregano, basil, salt and pepper in the slow cooker.
Make the meatballs by combining the ground turkey, egg, garlic powder, breadcrumbs, and Parmesan.
Form meatballs from the mixture.
Place a mozzarella ball in the center of each ball.
Add the meatballs in the slow cooker.
Seal the pot.
Cook on high for 3 hours.
Serving Suggestion:
Serve with spaghetti squash.
Tip:
Try using homemade breadcrumbs made from stale bread.
Nutrition:
Calories163
Fat 7g
Saturated Fat 3g
Fiber 2g
Carbohydrates 7g
Protein 14g
Cholesterol 69mg
Sugars 3g
Sodium 277mg
Potassium 506mg

Ranch Chicken

Preparation Time: 30 minutes
Cooking Time: 7 hours and 10 minutes

Servings: 6
Ingredients:
1 tablespoon dried minced onion
1 teaspoon garlic powder
2 teaspoons dried parsley flakes
1/2 teaspoon dried thyme
Salt and pepper to taste
2 onions, quartered
5 lb. chicken thighs, skin removed
10 oz. low fat, low sodium cream of chicken soup
8 oz. sour cream
3 teaspoons chipotle chili pepper in adobo sauce, chopped
2 green sweet pepper, sliced into strips
Directions:
In a bowl, mix the dried onion, garlic powder, parsley flakes, thyme, salt and pepper.
Sprinkle half of the mixture all over the chicken.
Place the onion quarters inside the slow cooker.
Add the chicken on top.
In another bowl, mix the soup, sour cream and chili peppers.
Pour this mixture over the chicken.
Seal the pot.
Cook on low for 7 hours.
Add the sweet pepper strips and squash.
Cover the pot.
Cook for 10 minutes.
Pour the sauce over the chicken before serving.
Serving Suggestion:
Use fresh parsley to garnish the dish.
Tip:
Use gloves when handling chili peppers.
Nutrition:
Calories291
Fat 10g
Saturated Fat 3g
Fiber 4g
Carbohydrates 20g
Protein 31g
Cholesterol 141mg
Sugars 9g

Sodium 494mg
Potassium 960mg

Rosemary Chicken

Preparation Time: 30 minutes
Cooking Time: 6 hours and 15 minutes
Servings: 6
Ingredients:
Cooking spray
1-1/2 lb. chicken breast (boneless, skinless)
1/2 cup onion, chopped
12 cloves garlic, minced
9 oz. frozen artichoke hearts
1/2 cup low sodium chicken broth
1 teaspoon lemon zest
1/2 teaspoon ground black pepper
2 teaspoons dried rosemary
1 tablespoon corn starch
1 tablespoon cold water
Directions:
Spray oil on a skillet.
Heat the skillet and brown the chicken.
In a slow cooker, add the onion, garlic and artichoke hearts.
In a bowl, mix the broth, lemon zest, pepper and rosemary.
Pour this mixture over the vegetables in the slow cooker.
Add the chicken.
Seal the pot.
Cook on low for 6 hours.
Transfer the chicken and vegetables on a serving plate.
Cover with foil.
In a bowl, mix the corn starch and water.
Add this to the liquid in the slow cooker.
Cover the pot and cook for 15 minutes.
Pour the sauce over the chicken and artichokes before serving.
Serving Suggestion:
Garnish with lemon wedges.
Tip:
Use freshly grated lemon zest.

Nutrition:
Calories172
Fat 3g
Saturated Fat 1g
Fiber 2g
Carbohydrates 8g
Protein 27g
Cholesterol 83mg
Sugars 1g
Sodium 108mg
Potassium 472mg

Turkey & Sweet Potatoes

Preparation Time: 15 minutes
Cooking Time: 5 hours and 20 minutes
Servings: 6
Ingredients:
6 turkey thighs, skin removed
2 lb. sweet potatoes, peeled and sliced into strips
1/2 lb. mushrooms, sliced
6 shallots, sliced in half
4 cloves garlic, peeled and crushed
2 teaspoons fresh rosemary, chopped
Salt and pepper to taste
Directions:
Place all the ingredients in the slow cooker.
Mix well.
Seal the pot.
Cook on low for 5 hours.
Shred the turkey and put it back to the slow cooker.
Cook for 10 more minutes.
Serving Suggestion:
Serve with Cole slaw.
Tip:
You can also stir in a teaspoon of white wine vinegar before serving.
Nutrition:
Calories300
Fat 6g

Saturated Fat 2g
Fiber 5g
Carbohydrates 38g
Protein 18g
Cholesterol 50mg
Sugars 8g
Sodium 520mg
Potassium 895mg

Beef, Pork, and Lamb Recipes

Your Go-To Barbecue Meatloaf

Preparation Time: 30 minutes
Cooking Time: 6 hours
Servings: 6
Ingredients:
2 pounds of lean ground beef
1 pound of lean ground pork
½ cup of onions, finely chopped
½ cup of almond flour
2 large eggs
1 cup of homemade zero-sugar barbecue sauce
1 teaspoon of sea salt
1 teaspoon of freshly cracked black pepper
1 teaspoon of garlic powder
Directions:
In a large bowl, add the ground beef, ground pork, onions, almond flour, eggs, salt, black pepper, and garlic powder. Stir until completely combined.
Form the meat mixture into a loaf and wrap using tin foil.
Place the meatloaf in your crockpot.
Cover and cook on Low for 5 to 6 hours.
Brush the barbecue sauce over the meatloaf.
Slice the meatloaf into servings.
Serve and enjoy!
Nutrition:
Calories: 370
Fat: 23g
Carbohydrates: 5g
Dietary Fiber: 2g
Protein: 27g

Superb Beef Stroganoff

Preparation Time: 30 minutes
Cooking Time: 6 hours
Servings: 6
Ingredients:
2 pounds of beef stew meat, cubed
4 (10.5-ounce) cans of cream of mushroom soup
1 cup of onions, chopped
2 tablespoons of Worcestershire sauce
½ cup of water
1 cup of coconut sour cream or paleo sour cream
2 teaspoons of minced garlic
Directions:
Stir all the ingredients in your crockpot until well combined.
Cover and cook on Low for 6 to 8 hours or until the meat is done.
Serve and enjoy!
Nutrition:
Calories: 442
Fat: 22.9g
Carbohydrates: 7.9g
Dietary Fiber: 0g
Protein: 48.6g

Fantastic Broccoli and Beef

Preparation Time: 30 minute
Cooking Time: 4 hours and 30 minutes
Servings: 6
Ingredients:
1 ½ pounds of sirloin steak, thinly sliced
2 cups of broccoli florets
1 cup of homemade low-sodium beef broth
½ cup of low-sodium coconut aminos
3 tablespoons of toasted sesame oil
1 tablespoon of sriracha sauce
3 garlic cloves, minced
3 green onions, thinly sliced

2 tablespoons of arrowroot powder
Toasted sesame seeds (for garnish)
Directions:
Add the thinly sliced sirloin steak, beef broth, coconut aminos, sesame oil, sriracha sauce, minced garlic, and thinly sliced green onions.
Cover and cook on low for 4 hours or until the beef is cooked through.
Transfer 2 tablespoons of the crockpot liquid to a bowl and stir with arrowroot powder.
Pour into the crockpot and stir until combined.
Add the broccoli.
Cover and cook for 20 minutes or more.
Garnish with sesame seeds and green onions.
Serve and enjoy!
Nutrition:
Calories: 309
Fat: 14g
Carbohydrates: 8.1g
Dietary Fiber: 1g
Protein: 35.4g

Crazy Honey Balsamic Beef

Preparation Time: 20 minutes
Cooking Time: 6 hours
Servings: 6
Ingredients:
4 pounds of boneless beef roast
1 medium onion, chopped
5 garlic cloves, minced
1 (14-ounce) can of sodium-reduced beef broth
½ cup of balsamic vinegar
2 tablespoons of low-sodium coconut aminos
2 tablespoons of Worcestershire sauce
3 tablespoons of pure organic honey
1 teaspoon of red chili flakes
½ teaspoon of sea salt
Directions:

Add all the ingredients to the crockpot and stir until fully combined. Cover and cook on Low for 6 to 8 hours.

When the cooking is done, remove the beef from the crockpot and shred using two forks.

Serve and enjoy!

Nutrition:

Calories: 581

Fat: 19.3g

Carbohydrates: 1.3g

Dietary Fiber: 0.1g

Protein: 93.3g

Exquisite Beef Bourguignon

Preparation Time: 40 minutes

Cooking Time: 8 hours

Servings: 8

Ingredients:

3 pounds of boneless beef chuck, cut into bite-sized pieces

1 pound of baby potatoes

6 bacon slices, finely chopped

1 cup of red cooking wine

2 cups of homemade low-sodium chicken broth

½ cup of tomato sauce

¼ cup of low-sodium coconut aminos

¼ cup of almond flour

3 garlic cloves, minced

1 cup of fresh mushrooms, sliced

2 tablespoons of fresh thyme, finely chopped

1 tablespoon of fresh parsley, finely chopped

5 medium carrots, sliced

½ teaspoon of sea salt

½ teaspoon of freshly cracked black pepper

Directions:

In a large skillet over medium-high heat, add the bacon bits and cook until brown and crispy.

Add the bacon bits to the crockpot.

Season the beef pieces with salt and black pepper. Add the beef to the skillet and cook until brown.

Transfer the beef to the crockpot.

Deglaze the skillet with the red cooking wine, scraping any browned bits on the bottom. Allow to simmer until reduced by half.

Add the chicken broth, tomato sauce, and coconut aminos. Slowly stir in the almond flour and allow to thicken.

Add the liquid to the crockpot along with the remaining ingredients. Gently stir until fully combined.

Cover and cook on Low for 8 to 10 hours or until tender. Serve and enjoy!

Nutrition:

Calories: 486

Fat: 17.7g

Carbohydrates: 16.9g

Dietary Fiber: 5.5g

Protein: 61.2g

Best Italian Beef and Pork Meatballs

Preparation Time: 30 minutes

Cooking Time: 6 hours

Servings: 6

Ingredients:

1 pound of ground beef

1 pound of ground pork

2 large eggs

1 onion, chopped

3 garlic cloves, minced

2 tablespoons of fresh parsley, chopped

2 (24-ounce) cans of crushed tomatoes

1 (6-ounce) cans of tomato paste

2 whole bay leaves

½ teaspoon of crushed red pepper flakes

½ teaspoon of Italian seasoning

1 teaspoon of salt

½ teaspoon of freshly cracked black pepper

Directions:

In a large bowl, add the ground beef, ground pork, onion, eggs, salt, and black pepper. Stir until well combined.

Form the meat mixture into meatballs.

Lightly grease a baking sheet with nonstick cooking spray and add the meatballs.

Place the baking sheet in your broiler and broil until brown.

Remove the meatballs from your broiler and add to your crockpot.

Top with the remaining ingredients.

Cover and cook on Low for 4 hours.

Serve and enjoy!

Nutrition:

Calories: 166

Fat: 9.2g

Carbohydrates: 7g

Dietary Fiber: 1.3g

Protein: 14g

Super Easy Beef Roast

Preparation Time: 30 minutes

Cooking Time: 8 hours and 30 minutes

Servings: 8

Ingredients:

3 pounds of boneless chuck roast

½ cup of homemade low-sodium beef broth

1 tablespoon of chives, chopped

2 tablespoons of fresh parsley, chopped

6 sweet potatoes or regular potatoes, peeled and cubed

5 medium carrots, peeled and cut into slices

1 large medium onion, quartered

2 tablespoons of Worcestershire sauce

1 (10-ounce) can cream of mushroom soup

½ teaspoon of garlic powder

½ teaspoon of onion powder

1 teaspoon of sea salt

1 teaspoon of freshly cracked black pepper

Directions:

Add the potatoes, carrots, and onions to the crockpot.

Add the boneless chuck roast on top of the vegetables.

Pour in the beef broth.

Add the chives, fresh parsley, Worcestershire sauce, cream of mushroom soup, garlic powder, onion powder, salt, and black pepper over the meat.

Cover and cook on Low for 8 to 10 hours.

Serve and enjoy!

Nutrition:

Calories: 477

Fat: 13g

Carbohydrates: 29g

Dietary Fiber: 5g

Protein: 38g

Beautiful Middle Eastern Lamb Stew

Preparation Time: 40 minutes

Cooking Time: 5 hours

Servings: 6

Ingredients:

2 pounds of boneless lamb stew meat

1 large yellow onion, finely chopped

1 medium sweet potato, cubed

1 zucchini, chopped

1 cup of baby carrots

1 green bell pepper, chopped

1 (28-ounce) can of diced tomatoes

2 cups of baby spinach

1 cup of homemade low-sodium chicken broth

4 garlic cloves, minced

2 tablespoons of canola oil

1 tablespoon of ground cumin

1 tablespoon of ground coriander

½ teaspoon of organic ground cayenne pepper

½ teaspoon of sea salt

½ teaspoon of freshly cracked black pepper

Directions:

In a small bowl, add the canola oil, garlic, ground cumin, ground coriander, ground cayenne pepper, salt, and black pepper. Mix well. Coat the lamb stew meat with the spice mixture

Add the lamb stew meat, diced tomatoes, chicken broth, minced garlic, and onion to your crockpot.
Cover and cook on High for 3 hours and 30 minutes.
Gently stir in the remaining ingredients.
Cover and cook on High until the spinach has wilted, typically around 5 minutes.
Serve and enjoy!
Nutrition:
Calories: 259
Fat: 15g
Carbohydrates: 13g
Dietary Fiber: 0.9g
Protein: 18g

The Tastiest Garlic Herbed Lamb Roast

Preparation Time: 30 minutes
Cooking Time: 8 hours and 30 minutes
Servings: 6
Ingredients:
4 pounds of boneless lamb roast
6 garlic cloves, thinly sliced
1 teaspoon of sea salt
2 tablespoons of canola oil
1 teaspoon of freshly cracked black pepper
1 teaspoon of fresh parsley
1 teaspoon of dried oregano
½ teaspoon of rosemary
Directions:
Use a knife to make a slit inside the lamb roast and stuff with the garlic.
In a bowl, add the sea salt, canola oil, black pepper, fresh parsley, dried oregano, and rosemary. Mix well and rub over the lamb roast.
Add the lamb roast to the crockpot.
Cover and cook on Low for 8 hours or until done.
Serve and enjoy!
Nutrition:
Calories: 608
Fat: 27.9g

Carbohydrates: 1g
Dietary Fiber: 0.1g
Protein: 85.1g

Lucky Mongolian Beef

Preparation Time: 30 minutes
Cooking Time: 8 hours and 15 minutes
Servings: 6
Ingredients:
2 pounds of beef chuck roast, trimmed of fat
½ cup of low-sodium coconut aminos
¼ cup of beef broth
3 garlic cloves, pressed
2 teaspoons of minced ginger
4 green onions, thinly sliced
1 tablespoon of canola oil
2 tablespoons of arrowroot powder
½ teaspoon of sea salt
½ teaspoon of freshly cracked black pepper
Directions:
Add the beef chuck roast, coconut aminos, beef broth, pressed garlic cloves, minced ginger to your crockpot.
Cover and cook on low for 8 to 10 hours.
Remove the meat from the liquid and transfer to a cutting board.
Shred using two forks and return to the crockpot.
In a small saucepan over medium heat, add ½ cup of the crockpot liquid with the arrowroot powder. Allow to thicken, whisking constantly.
Add the thickened liquid to the crockpot and stir until well combined.
Garnish with green onions.
Serve and enjoy!
Nutrition:
Calories: 318
Fat: 11.8g
Carbohydrates: 3.4g
Dietary Fiber: 0.3g
Protein: 46.1g

Contest-Winning Chili

Preparation Time: 30 minutes
Cooking Time: 4 hours and 30 minutes
Servings: 6
Ingredients:
1 pound of lean ground beef
1 pound of hot ground sausage
1 medium yellow onion, chopped
4 (14.5-ounce) cans of tomato sauce
1 (28-ounce) can of Mexican-style diced tomatoes
1 medium green bell pepper, chopped
1 (6-ounce) can of tomato paste
1 tablespoon of chili powder
½ tablespoon of ground cumin
4 garlic cloves, minced
1 teaspoon of salt
1 teaspoon of freshly cracked black pepper
Directions:
Brown the ground beef and ground sausage in a medium pan. Drain the liquid.
Add the browned beef and sausage to the crockpot.
Add the remaining ingredients to the crockpot and stir until well combined.
Cover and cook on Low for 6 to 8 hours.
Serve and enjoy!
Nutrition:
Calories: 519
Fat: 27.1g
Carbohydrates: 27.4g
Dietary Fiber: 7.2g
Protein: 44g

Family-Oriented Cuban Mojo Pork

Preparation Time: 20 minutes
Cooking Time: 8 hours
Servings: 8

Ingredients:
4 pounds of boneless pork shoulder
¼ cup of fresh orange juice
¼ cup of fresh lime juice
2 teaspoons of ground cumin
2 teaspoons of dried oregano
¼ teaspoon of crushed red pepper flakes
4 garlic cloves, minced
2 bay leaves
2 tablespoons of canola oil
2 teaspoons of sea salt
1 teaspoon of freshly cracked black pepper
½ teaspoon of freshly cracked black pepper
Directions:
Season the pork shoulder with salt and black pepper.
In a large pot over medium-high heat, add the canola oil.
Once hot, add the pork and brown on all sides.
Stir in the fresh orange juice, fresh lime juice, ground cumin, dried oregano, crushed red pepper flakes, minced garlic, and bay leaves to your crockpot.
Add the pork shoulder to the crockpot and roll until the mixture s well coated with the liquid.
Cover and cook on Low for 8 hours.
Once done, spoon the liquid on top of the pork.
Serve and enjoy!
Nutrition:
Calories: 361
Fat: 11.5g
Carbohydrates: 1.4g
Dietary Fiber: 0.1g
Protein: 59.5g

Awesome Sweet Apple Pork

Preparation Time: 40 minutes
Cooking Time: 8 hours
Servings: 6
Ingredients:
3 pounds of pork tenderloin

4 medium apples, wedged
½ cup of organic pure honey
2 tablespoons of ground cinnamon powder
1 medium cucumber
1 cup of cherry tomatoes
3 tablespoons of canola oil
2 teaspoons of red wine vinegar
1 teaspoon of Italian seasoning
¼ teaspoon of sea salt
¼ teaspoon of ground black pepper
Directions:
Make large slits in the pork tenderloin and stuff with apple wedges.
Add the remaining apple wedges to the crockpot and drizzle with ¼
cup of organic pure honey.
Spread the remaining ¼ cup of organic pure honey over the pork
tenderloin and sprinkle with cinnamon.
Cover and cook on Low for 6 to 8 hours.
Serve and enjoy!
Nutrition:
Calories: 683
Fat: 21g
Carbohydrates: 60g
Dietary Fiber: 5g
Protein: 35g

Flavorful Moroccan Lamb

Preparation Time: 30 minutes
Cooking Time: 2 hours
Servings: 6
Ingredients:
2 ½ pounds of boned lamb shoulder, well-trimmed and cut into bite-
sized pieces
1 tablespoon of organic ground cumin
2 teaspoons of organic ground coriander
1 teaspoon of fennel seeds
½ teaspoon of organic ground cayenne pepper
1 teaspoon of sea salt
1 teaspoon of freshly cracked black pepper

4 tablespoons of canola oil, divided
1 large onion, finely chopped
2 tablespoons of organic ground tomato paste
2 cups of homemade low-sodium chicken stock
2 large plum tomatoes, chopped
2 cinnamon sticks
1 tablespoon of freshly minced ginger
2 teaspoons of lemon zest
1 (15.5) ounce can of chickpeas, drained
1 cup of dried apricots
¼ cup of fresh cilantro, chopped
Directions:
In a small bowl, add the ground cumin, salt, black pepper, fennel seeds, ground coriander, cayenne pepper, Mix well.
Season the lamb with the spice mixture.
In a heavy large skillet over medium-high heat, add 2 tablespoons of canola oil.
Working in batches, add the lamb and cook until brown on all sides, stirring occasionally.
Add the additional tablespoon of olive oil to the skillet to the next batch.
Transfer all the lamb to a large bowl.
Add the onions, tomato paste, chicken stock, and plum tomatoes, cinnamon sticks, minced ginger, lemon zest, chickpeas, and dried apricots to your crockpot.
Cover and cook on Low for 1 hour.
Remove the lid and simmer until the sauce thickens, stirring occasionally.
Serve and enjoy!
Nutrition:
Calories: 753
Fat: 52g
Carbohydrates: 13g
Dietary Fiber: 6.9g
Protein: 33g

Good Roasted Leg of Lamb

Preparation Time: 30 minutes

Cooking Time: 7 hours and 30 minutes

Servings: 6

Ingredients:

1 (3-pound) bone-in leg of lamb

1 cup of dry red wine

¼ cup of ghee or canola oil

1 lemon, juiced

2 tablespoons of organic Dijon mustard

4 garlic cloves, minced

1 tablespoon of apple cider vinegar

1 tablespoon of dried rosemary

1 teaspoon of dried thyme

1 teaspoon of paprika

1 teaspoon of sea salt

1 teaspoon of freshly cracked black pepper

Directions:

Stir in the red wine, ghee, lemon juice, Dijon mustard, garlic, apple cider vinegar, dried rosemary, dried thyme, paprika, sea salt, and freshly cracked black pepper.

Add the lamb to the crockpot stoneware.

Cover and cook on Low for 5 hours.

When the lamb is cooked through, allow the lamb to rest for 20 minutes.

Serve and enjoy!

Nutrition:

Calories: 542

Fat: 25.9g

Carbohydrates: 2g

Dietary Fiber: 0.2g

Protein: 64.1g

Fish and Seafood Recipes

Terrific Seafood Gumbo with Prawns

Preparation Time: 40 minutes
Cooking Time: 7 hours
Servings: 8
Ingredients:
24-ounces of sea bass fillets, cut into bite-sized pieces
2 pounds of prawns, deveined
1 ½ cup of homemade low-sodium fish stock or bone broth
¼ cup of organic tomato paste
1 (28-ounce) can of organic diced tomatoes
4 celery ribs, finely chopped
2 medium-sized bell peppers, seeded and finely chopped
2 medium-sized yellow onions, finely chopped
3 tablespoons of Cajun seasoning
3 tablespoons of organic ghee
1 teaspoon of sea salt
1 teaspoon of freshly cracked black pepper
Directions:
Season the fish fillets with salt, black pepper, and ½ of the Cajun seasoning.
Place a skillet over medium-high heat and add the ghee. Once the ghee has melted, add the sea bass fillet chunks and sauté for 4 minutes.
Stir in the remaining Cajun seasoning, celery, bell peppers, and yellow onions to the skillet and sauté for 2 minutes or until fragrant, stirring frequently. Remove from the heat and add to your crockpot.
Add the prawns, fish stock, tomato paste, and diced tomatoes to your Instant Pot.
Cover your crockpot with the lid and set for 7 hours on low setting.
Serve and enjoy!
Nutrition:
Calories: 320
Fat: 9.2g

Carbohydrates: 10g
Dietary Fiber: 2.3g
Protein: 47.6g

Asian-Inspired Braised Squid

Preparation Time: 40 minutes
Cooking Time: 7 hours
Servings: 6
Ingredients:
1 pound of squid rings
1 (2-inch) ginger, finely minced
2 leeks stalks, thinly sliced
2 bay leaves
½ teaspoon of sea salt
½ teaspoon of freshly cracked black pepper
5 garlic cloves, crushed
1 tablespoon of sesame oil
¼ cup of low-sodium coconut aminos
¼ cup of oyster sauce
¼ cup of Chinese cooking white
Directions:
Add all the ingredients to your crockpot and gently stir until well combined.
Cover and cook on Low for 8 hours.
Serve and enjoy!
Nutrition:
Calories: 122
Fat: 6g
Carbohydrates: 4.94g
Dietary Fiber: 0.2g
Protein: 12.22g

Excellent Soy-Singer Steamed Pompano

Preparation Time: 20 minutes
Cooking Time: 1 hour

Servings: 6
Ingredients:
1 whole pompano fish
¼ cup of low-sodium coconut aminos
¼ cup of toasted sesame oil
¼ cup of Chinese cooking wine
1 (2-inch) piece of ginger, thinly sliced
6 garlic cloves, crushed
1 bunch of leeks, finely chopped
1 bunch of fresh cilantro, roughly chopped
Directions:
Prepare the whole pompano fish by scaling, gutting, and making diagonal cuts on both sides of the fish.
In a bowl, add and combine the coconut aminos, sesame oil, Chinese cooking wine, ginger, garlic.
Lay the leeks to the bottom of your crockpot and place the whole fish on top.
Add the coconut amino mixture over the whole fish.
Cover and cook on High for 1 hour.
Serve and enjoy!
Nutrition:
Calories: 185
Fat: 13.8g
Carbohydrates: 1g
Dietary Fiber: 0.1g
Protein: 14.9g

Celebratory Lobster Chowder

Preparation Time: 40 minutes
Cooking Time: 5 hours
Servings: 12
Ingredients:
3 cups of sweet potatoes, peeled and cubed
¾ cups of onions, finely chopped
1 ½ pounds of cooked lobster meat, cut into bite-sized pieces
½ teaspoon of smoked paprika
½ teaspoon of ground cumin
1 teaspoon of fresh thyme

1 teaspoon of sea salt
1 teaspoon of basil
½ teaspoon of white pepper
1 teaspoon of garlic powder
¼ cup of coconut flour or almond flour
4 bacon slices, chopped
1 medium jalapeno, finely chopped
1 ½ cup of organic low-sodium lobster stock
3 ½ cup of organic coconut cream or non-dairy half-and-half
Directions:
Add all the ingredients except for the bacon and lobster to your crockpot. Gently stir until well combined.
In a skillet over medium-high heat, add the bacon and cook until brown and crispy. Add the bacon and bacon grease to your crockpot. Cover and cook on High for 5 hours or on Low for 10 hours.
Stir in the lobster meat and gently stir until well combined. Cover and continue to cook.
Nutrition:
Calories: 534
Fat: 55.13g
Carbohydrates: 6.36g
Dietary Fiber: 2.2g
Protein: 7.03g

Booming Seabass in Flavorful Coconut Cream Sauce

Preparation Time: 30 minutes
Cooking Time: 1 hour and 30 minutes
Servings: 2
Ingredients:
1 sea bass
5 medium jalapeno peppers, sliced
4 stalks of bok choy
1 tablespoon of fish sauce
2 cups of unsweetened coconut cream
2 scallion stalks, thinly sliced
1 2-inch ginger, thinly sliced

Directions:
In a bowl, add the jalapenos, coconut cream, fish sauce, scallion, and ginger to the bottom of your crockpot.
Place the seabass on top.
Lay the bok choy stalks on top of the seabass.
Cover and cook on High for 1 hour and 30 minutes.
Serve and enjoy!
Nutrition:
Calories: 532
Fat: 55.3g
Carbohydrates: 27.1g
Dietary Fiber: 6.3g
Protein: 62.3g

Great Seafood Cioppino

Preparation Time: 30 minutes
Cooking Time: 8
Servings: 4
Ingredients:
1 pound of haddock fillets, cut into bite-sized pieces
1 pound of shrimp, peeled and deveined
2 tablespoons of fresh parsley, finely chopped
1 (6-ounce) can of crabmeat, drained
1 (6-ounce) can of chopped clams, undrained
1 (28-ounce) can of crushed tomatoes, undrained
1 (8-ounce) bottle of clam juice
1 (6-ounce) can of tomato paste
½ cup of dry white wine
6 garlic cloves, minced
1 tablespoon of canola oil or olive oil
2 teaspoons of Italian seasoning
2 medium-sized yellow onions, finely chopped
3 fresh celery ribs, finely chopped
1 tablespoon of fresh parsley, finely chopped
1 bay leaf
1 teaspoon of sea salt
1 teaspoon of freshly cracked black pepper
Directions:

Add the crushed tomatoes, onions, celery, clam juice, tomato paste, white wine, minced garlic, canola oil, Italian seasoning, bay leaf, parsley, salt, and black pepper to your crockpot.
Cover and cook on Low for 4 to 5 hours.
Gently stir in the haddock fillet pieces, shrimp, chopped clams, and crabmeat to your crockpot.
Cover and cook on High for 20 to 30 minutes or until the shrimp becomes pink and opaque.
Remove the bay leaf.
Serve and enjoy!
Nutrition:
Calories: 207
Fat: 4g
Carbohydrates: 16g
Dietary Fiber: 4g
Protein: 31g

Awesome Clams with Tomatoes and Bacon

Preparation Time: 25 minutes
Cooking Time: 2 hours
Servings: 6
Ingredients:
6 slices of bacon, cut into bite-sized pieces
1 medium yellow onion, finely chopped
1 teaspoon of dried oregano
1 (14.5-ounce) can of diced tomatoes, undrained
1 (8-ounce) bottle of clam juice
3 tablespoons of capers with liquid
24 clams, cleaned
1 teaspoon of sea salt
1 teaspoon of freshly cracked black pepper
Directions:
In a skillet over medium-high heat, add the bacon and cook until brown. Remove and set aside.
Add the onions to the bacon grease and sauté for 1 minute.
Add the oregano and sauté for an extra 2 minutes, stirring occasionally.
Add the onion and bacon to the stoneware of your crockpot.

Gently stir in the diced tomatoes, capers with liquid, clam juice, salt, and black pepper.

Cover with the glass lid and cook on Low for 3 hours.

Add the clams and cover with the glass lid and cook on High for 30 minutes.

Serve and enjoy!

Nutrition:

Calories: 185

Fat: 13.8g

Carbohydrates: 1g

Dietary Fiber: 0.1g

Protein: 14.9g

Occasional Lemon and Dill Salmon

Preparation Time: 20 minutes

Cooking Time: 1 hour

Servings: 2

Ingredients:

2 pounds of salmon

2 garlic cloves, minced

1 tablespoon of fresh dill

1 medium-sized lemon, sliced

1 teaspoon of olive oil

1 teaspoon of salt

1 teaspoon of freshly cracked black pepper

Directions:

Grease your crockpot with nonstick cooking spray or line with parchment paper.

Drizzle the salmon with olive oil and season with salt, black pepper, dill, and garlic.

Add the salmon to the crockpot and top with lemon slices.

Cover and cook on High for 1 hour.

Serve and enjoy!

Nutrition:

Calories: 629

Fat: 30.4g

Carbohydrates: 1.9g

Dietary Fiber: 0.3g

Protein: 88.5g

New-England Style Shrimp Boil

Preparation Time: 30 minutes
Cooking Time: 5 hours
Servings: 8
Ingredients:
4 tablespoons of old bay seafood seasoning
3 pounds of sweet potatoes, cut into bite-sized pieces
8-ounces of kielbasa sausage, cut into slices
4 garlic cloves, crushed
2 medium-sized yellow onions, finely chopped
½ cup of fresh parsley, finely chopped
¼ cup of fresh lemon juice
2 bay leaves
1 ½ pounds of large shrimp pieces, deveined
2 large yellow corn ears, husked and cut into bite-sized pieces
4 cups of seafood stock or water
1 teaspoon of salt
1 teaspoon of freshly cracked black pepper
Directions:
Add the sweet potatoes, crushed garlic, bay leaves, onions, and 4 cups of water or seafood stock to your crockpot.
Cover and cook on Low for 4 hours.
Remove the glass lid and gently stir in the remaining ingredients.
Cover and cook on High for 30 to 45 minutes.
Serve and enjoy!
Nutrition:
Calories: 229
Fat: 6.32g
Carbohydrates: 31.61g
Dietary Fiber: 4.5g
Protein: 13.59g

Fabulous Salmon Curry

Preparation Time: 30 minutes
Cooking Time: 3 hours and 30 minutes
Servings: 6
Ingredients:
6 boneless skinless salmon fillets
1 (12-ounce) can of pureed tomatoes
1 medium yellow onion, finely chopped
6 garlic cloves, minced
2 teaspoons of fresh ginger, grated
3 celery stalks, chopped
2 medium carrots, chopped
2 cans of unsweetened coconut milk
½ cup of homemade low-sodium fish stock
1 teaspoon of coriander
1 teaspoon of ground cumin
1 teaspoon of chili powder
2 teaspoons of paprika
1 teaspoon of turmeric
½ teaspoon of sea salt
½ teaspoon of freshly cracked black pepper
¼ cup of fresh cilantro, finely chopped (for garnishing)
Directions:
Add all the ingredients to your instant pot except for the cilantro, coconut milk, and salmon. Gently stir until well combined.
Lay the salmon on top.
Cover and cook on Low for 2 hours.
Remove the lid and stir in the coconut milk and cook on High for 1 hour.
Garnish with fresh cilantro.
Serve and enjoy!
Nutrition:
Calories: 523
Fat: 38.2g
Carbohydrates: 12.5g
Dietary Fiber: 4.2g
Protein: 38.1g

Appetizers

Lovely Baked Eggs

Preparation Time: 10 minutes
Cooking Time: 4 minutes
Servings: 4
Ingredients:
4 whole eggs
4 slices low-fat cheddar
2 spring onions, chopped
1 tablespoon olive oil
1 tablespoon cilantro, chopped
1 cup water
Directions:
Take 4 ramekins and grease them with oil
Sprinkle green onion in each
Crack and egg into each ramekin and top with cilantro and cheddar
Place a steamer basket in your pot
Place ramekin in the basket and lock lid
Cook on LOW pressure for 4 minutes
Release pressure naturally over 10 minutes
Serve and enjoy!
Nutrition:
Calories: 211
Fat: 3g
Carbohydrates: 18g
Protein: 5g

Hot Pickled Green Chilies

Preparation Time: 2 minutes
Cooking Time: 4 minutes
Servings: 8
Ingredients:
1 pound green chilies, sliced

1 teaspoon canning salt
1/4 teaspoon garlic powder
1 and 1/2 cups apple cider vinegar
1 and 1/2 teaspoons stevia
Directions:
Add the listed ingredients to Instant Pot
Stir and lock lid
Cook on HIGH pressure for 4 minutes
Quick release pressure
Serve and enjoy!
Nutrition:
Calories: 3.1
Fat: 0g
Carbohydrates: 0.6g
Protein: 0.1g

Outstanding Creamy Garlic, Artichoke and Zucchini

Preparation Time: 1 minutes
Cooking Time: 10 minutes
Servings: 12
Ingredients:
2 tablespoons coconut oil
1 bulb garlic, minced
1 large artichoke hearts, cleaned and sliced
2 medium zucchinis, sliced
1/2 cup cashew cream
1/2 cup vegetable broth
Salt and pepper to taste
Directions:
Set your pot to Sauté mode and add oil, let it heat up
Add garlic and Sauté until fragrant
Add remaining ingredients and lock lid
Cook on HIGH pressure for 10 minutes
Quick release pressure
Enjoy!
Nutrition:

Calories: 33
Fat: 0.57g
Carbohydrates: 1.7g
Protein: 0.57g

Soft and Tender Baked Potato

Preparation Time: 5 minutes
Cooking Time: 20 minutes
Servings: 4
Ingredients:
1 cup water
2 pounds medium baking potatoes, washed and scrubbed
Directions:
Wash potatoes thoroughly and place them in the Instant Pot
Pierce the sides of the potatoes using fork
Add a cup of water
Pre-heat your oven to 450 degree F
Lock lid and cook on HIGH pressure for 10 minutes
Release pressure naturally over 10 minutes
Use tongs to take the potatoes out and place them in the middle rack of your oven
Bake for 10-15 minutes
Serve baked potatoes and enjoy!
Nutrition:
Calories: 150
Fat: 0g
Carbohydrates: 39g
Protein: 6g

Classy Brussels with Pine Nuts

Preparation Time: 2 minutes
Cooking Time: 5 minutes
Servings: 6
Ingredients:
1 pound Brussels sprouts, trimmed and cleaned

1/4 cup pine nuts, toasted
1 pomegranate, seeds saved
1 tablespoon olive oil
Salt and pepper to taste
Directions:
Place a trivet inside your pot
Add a cup of water
Place Brussels on trivet
Lock lid and cook on STEAM mode on default settings
Naturally release pressure over 10 minutes
Transfer Brussels to salad bowl
Add remaining ingredients to Brussels and toss
Serve and enjoy!
Nutrition:
Calories: 132
Fat: 7g
Carbohydrates: 17g
Protein: 05g

Cool Chives and Garlic Potato Mash

Preparation Time: 8 minute
Cooking Time: 8 minutes
Servings: 5
Ingredients:
2 cups vegetable stock
2 pounds Yukon potatoes, peeled
4 garlic cloves, peeled
1/2 cup almond milk
1/2 teaspoon salt
1/4 cup chives, chopped
Directions:
Add broth, potatoes and garlic to the pot
Lock up the lid and cook on HIGH pressure for 9 minutes
Release the pressure naturally
Drain the amount of liquid need for your desired consistency
Mash the potatoes and stir in milk and salt
Stir in chives and serve!
Nutrition:

Calories: 293
Fat: 14g
Carbohydrates: 35g
Protein: 8g

Tender Soft Sticky Carrot

Preparation Time: 2 minutes
Cooking Time: 10 minutes
Servings: 8
Ingredients:
2 pounds carrots, peeled and thickly sliced
1/4 cup raisins
1 tablespoons clarified butter, melted
1 tablespoon stevia
Pepper to taste
Directions:
Add carrots and raisins to the Instant Pot
Add a cup of water to the pot and lock lid
Cook on STEAM mode for 6 minutes
Drain carrots and raisins and remove excess water
1Set your pot to Sauté mode and heat butter, stevia and add the carrots back to the pot
1Season with pepper
1Let it simmer for 2 minutes
1Serve and enjoy!
Nutrition:
Calories: 63
Fat: 2g
Carbohydrates: 11g
Protein: 1g

Mind-Blowing Guacamole

Preparation Time: 5 minutes
Cooking Time: 5 minutes
Servings: 6

Ingredients:
1 large avocado, cubed
1/4 red onion, chopped
1/2 a lime, juice
1 sprig cilantro, chopped
1 pinch salt
Directions:
Halve avocado vertically and gently remove the pit
Run a knife vertically and horizontally into the flesh
Take a spoon and scoop out cubed avocado pieces from the skin
Place in a small bowl
Take a fork and mash avocado
Mix in lime juice, lime, onion, salt and cilantro
Serve and enjoy!
Nutrition:
Calories: 50
Fat: 5g
Carbohydrates: 3g
Protein: 0.7g

Enjoyable Rosemary Garlic Potatoes

Preparation Time: 2 minutes
Cooking Time: 30 minutes
Servings: 4
Ingredients:
1 pound potatoes, peeled and sliced
2 garlic cloves
1/2 teaspoon salt
1 tablespoon olive oil
2 sprigs rosemary
Directions:
Place a trivet in Instant Pot and add water
Take a baking dish (small enough to fit in pot) and add the listed
ingredients, toss
Cover with aluminum foil and place on baking dish
Lock lid and cook on STEAM button for 30 minutes
Quick release pressure
Serve and enjoy!

Nutrition:
Calories: 119
Fat: 4g
Carbohydrates: 20g
Protein: 2g

The Major Beets in a Pot

Preparation Time: 5 minutes
Cooking Time: 15 minutes
Servings: 6
Ingredients:
6 medium sized beets
1 cup water
Salt and pepper as needed
Balsamic vinegar
Extra virgin olive oil
Directions:
Wash beets and trim them to ½ inch long portions
Add a cup of water to Instant Pot
Place a steamer insert on top of your Instant Pot
Arrange beats in the steamer insert
Lock lid and cook on HIGH pressure for 15 minutes, release
pressure naturally over 10 minutes
Open lid and let the beets cool
Slice the tops and slide the skin off
Slice beets to uniform portions and season with salt and pepper
Add a splash of vinegar and let them marinate for 30 minutes
Add extra virgin olive oil
1Serve and enjoy!
Nutrition:
Calories: 24
Fat: 0g
Carbohydrates: 5g
Protein: 1g

Desserts

Italian Raspberry-Coconut Cake

Preparation Time: 10 minutes
Cooking Time: 20 minutes
Servings: 6
Ingredients:
2 cups flaxseed meal
1 cup almond meal
½ cup melted butter
2 cups fresh raspberries, mashed + extra for topping
1 lemon, juiced
1 cup coconut cream
1 cup unsweetened coconut flakes
1 cup whipping cream
Directions:
Preheat the oven to 400 F.
In a medium bowl, mix the flaxseed meal, almond meal, and butter.
Spread the mixture in the bottom of a small baking dish. Bake in the
oven for 20 minutes until the mixture is crusty.
Remove the dish from the oven and allow cooling.
In another bowl, mix the raspberries with the lemon juice. Spread the
mixture on the crust.
Carefully, spread the coconut cream on top, scatter with the coconut
flakes and add the whipped cream all over.
Garnish with 10 to 12 raspberries and chill in the refrigerator for at
least 2 hours.
Serve afterwards.
Nutrition:
Calories 556;
Fats 55g;
Net Carbs 10g;
Protein 32g

Balsamic Strawberry Ricotta

Alternately, layer your favorite keto fruit with ricotta cheese on a dessert plate. Add some tang and sweetness, and enjoy. That simple!
Preparation Time: 4 minutes
Cooking Time: 0 minutes
Servings: 4
Ingredients:
2 cups fresh strawberries, chopped
1 cup ricotta cheese
2 tbsp. sugar-free maple syrup
2 tbsp. balsamic vinegar
Directions:
Divide half of the strawberries onto 4 dessert plates and top with the ricotta cheese.
Drizzle with the maple syrup, balsamic vinegar and top with the remaining strawberries.
Serve immediately.
Nutrition:
Calories 164;
Fats 8g;
Net Carbs 8g;
Protein 7g

Blueberry Sorbet

Since we can't have regular ice cream on the keto diet, we will have some sorbet instead! And this one rocks!
Preparation Time: 15 minutes + 6 hours chilling
Cooking Time: 0 minutes
Servings: 4
Ingredients:
4 cups frozen blueberries
1 cup swerve sugar
½ lemon, juiced
½ tsp salt
Directions:

In a blender, add the blueberries, swerve sugar, lemon juice, and salt. Process until smooth. Strain the mixture through a colander into a bowl. Chill for 2 to 3 hours.

Pour the chilled juice into an ice cream maker and churn until the mixture resembles ice cream.

Spoon into a bowl and chill further for 3 hours.

Serve when ready to enjoy.

Nutrition:

Calories 178;

Fats 1g;

Net Carbs 2.3g;

Protein 1g

Strawberry Mousse

I saved one of the bests for the last, and it is my favorite dessert-in-a-glass recipes. You can swap the berries based on your preference, and it will turn out fantastic too.

Preparation Time: 10 minutes + 2 hours chilling

Cooking Time: 0 minutes

Servings: 4

Ingredients:

2 ½ cups frozen strawberries + more for garnishing

2 tbsp. swerve sugar

1 large egg white

2 cups whipped cream

Directions:

Pour the strawberries into a blender and process until smooth.

Add the swerve sugar and process further. Pour in the egg white and blend until well combined.

Pour the mixture into a medium bowl and use an electric hand mixer to whisk until fluffy.

Spoon the mixture into dessert glasses, top with the whipped cream and then, some strawberries.

Chill for 2 hours and serve afterwards.

Nutrition:

Calories 145;

Fats 7g;

Net Carbs 4.8g;

Protein 2g

Sweet Lemon Panna Cotta

Talk of the Italian cuisine and panna cotta has to be involved. Here is my favorite one.

Preparation Time: 30 minutes + 7 hours chilling
Cooking Time: 0 minutes
Servings: 4
Ingredients:
½ cup coconut milk
1 cup heavy cream
¼ cup swerve sugar
5 tbsp. sugar-free maple syrup
3 tsp agar agar
¼ cup warm water
3 tbsp. water
½ lemon, juiced
Directions:
Heat the coconut milk and heavy cream in a medium pot over low heat.
Stir in the swerve sugar, 3 tablespoons of the maple syrup, and 2 teaspoons of the agar agar. Continue cooking for 2 to 3 minutes.
Cool completely and divide the mixture into 4 dessert cups. Chill in the refrigerator for 5 hours or until set.
In a medium bowl, soak the remaining agar agar with the warm water. Allow blooming for 5 minutes.
In a small pot, heat 3 tbsp. of water with the lemon juice. Mix in the remaining maple syrup and add the agar mixture. Continually whisking while cooking until no lumps form.
Turn the heat off and cool for 2 minutes.
Remove the dessert cups, pour in the mixture and refrigerate further for 2 hours.
When ready to serve, take out the cups, allow sitting for 15 minutes and then enjoy afterwards.
Nutrition:
Calories 208;
Fats 18g;
Net Carbs 2.8g;

Protein 2g

Fudgy Macadamia Chocolate Fat Bomb

Preparation Time: 5 minutes
Cooking Time: 0 minutes
Servings: 6
Ingredients:
¼ cup of coconut oil or heavy cream
112g (4 oz.) chopped macadamias
2 tablespoons of Swerve
2 tablespoons of unsweetened cocoa powder
58g (2 oz.) cocoa butter
Directions:
In a small saucepan, melt the cocoa butter in a bath of water
Add the cocoa powder to the melted butter then add the swerve and
mix well until the ingredients are melted and well blended.
Add the macadamias and stir them in well.
Add the coconut oil or the heavy cream and mix well then bring
back to room temperature.
Pour the mixture in paper candy cups or molds and leave to cool
before placing in the fridge to harden.
Nutrition:
Calorie: 267;
Protein: 3g;
Carbohydrates: 3g;
Fat: 28g

Low Carb Pecan Fudge Fat Bombs

Preparation Time: 10 minutes
Cooking Time: 0 minutes
Servings: 10
Ingredients:
½ cup of pecans, chopped roughly
1/3 cup of heavy cream
4 tablespoons of Swerve

4 tablespoons of unsweetened cocoa powder
½ cup of coconut oil
4 oz. cocoa powder, food grade
Silicone molds
Directions:
Melt the coconut oil and the cocoa butter over a double boiler.
Add the cocoa powder and whisk until there are no clumps.
Pour the mixture into a blender and add the swerve then blend for 1-2 minutes.
Add the heavy cream and blend for around 5 minutes. This will ensure that the sugar dissolves.
Place the silicone molds on a sheet pan and fill them halfway through with pecans.
Pour the mixture into the molds and chill for 4 hours in the refrigerator.
Pop the fat bombs out of the molds and enjoy.
Nutrition:
Calories: 140;
Protein: 2g;
Carbohydrates: 3g;
Fat: 15.3g

Easter egg Cookie Dough Fat Bombs

Preparation Time: 30 minutes
Cooking Time: 20 minutes
Servings: 14
Ingredients:
1/3 cup (235g) of sugar-free dark chocolate chips
¼ teaspoon of gray sea salt
5-10 drops of alcohol-free stevia
1 teaspoon of alcohol-free vanilla extract
½ cup of coconut oil
(70g) of almond flour
Coating
Easter-themed natural food coloring
½ cup (112g) of coconut butter, melted
Directions:

Line a large baking sheet with silicone baking mat or parchment paper

Add the stevia, vanilla, salt, coconut oil and almond flour to a food processor with an "s" blade and process for about 20 seconds until smooth.

Fold in the sugar-free chocolate chips. Scoop out 1.5 tablespoons of the mixture and roll into a ball in between your palms. Place on the earlier prepared baking sheet and flatten to the shape of a large egg. Repeat this procedure with the remaining dough.

Place the baking sheet in the freezer to chill for an hour.

Prepare a cooling rack by placing it over the top of another separate baking sheet and set aside.

Making the frosting

Melt the coconut butter and divide into separate dishes then add the Easter egg-themed food coloring.

Once the cookie dough eggs are ready, remove from freezer. Dip only 1 side of each cookie dough egg into the melted coconut butter and place on the earlier prepared cooling rack.

Add the colored coconut butter to a Ziploc bag then cut out the tip and sprinkle over the top of the "eggs."

Transfer the cooling rack with the colored eggs to the refrigerator and leave to set for 1 hour.

You can store them in a sealed container in the fridge for up to 5 days or freeze them and enjoy for a month.

Nutrition:

Calories: 161;

Protein: 1.8g;

Carbohydrates: 5.8g;

Fat: 15.9g

Chocolate Chip Fat Bombs

Preparation Time: 10 minutes

Cooking Time: 10 minutes

Servings: 9

Ingredients:

¼ cup of sugar-free chocolate chips

¾ cup of heavy cream or coconut milk

½ teaspoon of vanilla extract

¼ teaspoon of sea salt
½ cup of grass-fed butter or coconut oil or ghee, melted
¼ cup of swerve
Directions:
In a large bowl, combine the coconut flour, vanilla, butter, salt,
swerve and heavy cream (or coconut milk) until well blended.
Fold in the chocolate chips.
Place in the refrigerator to set for 1 hour.
Remove from fridge and roll into balls.
Place in a container to store in the freezer and enjoy one at a time.
Nutrition:
Calories: 165;
Protein: 1.1g;
Carbohydrates: 6.7g;
Fat: 5.2g

Easy Chocolate Fat Bombs with Coconut Oil

Preparation Time: 10 minutes
Cooking Time: 0 minutes
Servings: 20
Ingredients:
¼ cup of cocoa powder
1/3 cup of powdered monk fruit sweetener
Tablespoons of coconut oil, measured in a solid form then melted
2 tablespoons of MCT oil (or more coconut oil)
2 cups of macadamia nuts, roasted dry and salted
Optional:
1 teaspoon of vanilla extract
Directions:
Puree/pulse the macadamia nuts in a food processor or a high-power
blender until the nuts are mostly broken down into small bits.
Add the vanilla, melted coconut oil and MCT oil then continue to
blend until you form nut butter—try to get the butter smooth, but it's
also fine if you can't get rid of stray pieces. Scrape down the nuts on
the sides if any.
Gradually add the sweetener and the cacao powder, a few
tablespoons at a time and puree after every addition until smooth

Prepare a mini muffin pan by lining it with parchment liners. Spoon or pour the batter onto each liner evenly until about 1/3 of the way full.

Freeze the chocolate fat bombs until solid for at least 30 minutes.

Nutrition:

Calories 122,

Proteins 1g,

Carbs 2g

Fats 13g

White Chocolate Fat Bombs

Preparation Time: 5 minutes

Cooking Time: 10 minutes

Servings: 8

Ingredients:

10 drops of vanilla stevia drops

¼ cup (35g) of coconut oil

¼ cup (25g) of cocoa butter

Directions:

Place the coconut oil and cocoa butter in a double boiler and melt together over low heat.

Remove from heat then add in the vanilla flavored stevia drops and stir.

Pour the mixture into molds and chill until hardened.

Remove the fat bombs from molds and enjoy.

Store in refrigerator.

Nutrition:

Calories: 125;

Protein: 0g;

Carbohydrates: 0g;

Fat: 10g

White Chocolate Raspberry Fat Bombs

Preparation Time: 5 minutes + 1 hour chilling time

Cooking Time: 0 minutes

Servings: 10-12
Ingredients:
1/4 cup of powdered erythritol sweetener (such as Swerve)
1/2 cup of freeze-dried raspberries
2 ounces of cacao butter
1/2 cup of coconut oil
Directions:
Prepare a 12-cup muffin pan by lining with paper liners or just use a silicone muffin pan.
In a small pan, heat the cacao butter and the coconut oil over low heat until they completely melt then remove the pan from heat
Place the freeze-dried raspberries in a coffee grinder, blender or food processor and grind.
Add the powdered erythritol and the pulverized berries to the small saucepan and stir until the erythritol is mostly dissolved.
Distribute the mixture evenly among the muffin cups. The berry powder will sink to the bottom of the muffin pan—no worry. Just ensure that as you pour the mixture into each mold, you stir it first so that each gets some raspberry powder.
Chill until firm for 1 hour. You can store in the refrigerator for several weeks.
Nutrition:
Calories: 153;
Protein: 0.2g;
Carbohydrates: 1.2g;
Fat: 16.6g

Chocolate Cherry Fat Bombs

Preparation Time: 10 minutes
Cooking Time: 0 minutes
Servings: 12
Ingredients:
¾ cup of frozen dark sweet cherries, thawed
½ teaspoon of vanilla extract
½ teaspoon of almond extract
5 drops of stevia
3 tablespoons of cacao powder
¼ cup of cocoa butter, melted

¼ cup of coconut oil, melted

Directions:

Mix all ingredients apart from the dark berries.

Mash the dark cherries with a fork once they have thawed then mix them together with their juices in the chocolate mix.

Use a tablespoon to spoon a tablespoonful into an ice cube tray or mini cupcake liners. Freeze for 1 hour or longer.

Store in the fridge.

Nutrition:

Calories: 67;

Protein: 0g;

Carbohydrates: 2g;

Fat: 6g

Condiments, Sauces and Spreads Recipes

Spinach Crab Dip

Preparation Time: 5 minutes

Cooking Time: 20 minutes + releasing

Servings: 8

Ingredients:

2 tbsp. unsalted butter

1 red onion (minced)

1 tbsp. of minced garlic

¼ cup almond flour

¼ cup coconut milk

1/3 cup mayonnaise

¼ cup nutritional yeast

8 ounces chopped frozen spinach (drained)

1 tsp Italian seasoning

1 bay leaf

1 lime (juiced)

6 ounces crab meat (drained)

½ tsp sea salt or to taste

¼ tsp red pepper flakes

2 green medium onions (chopped)

Directions:

Select the sauté function on your instant pot and leave the pot to heat until it indicates HOT.

Add 1 tbsp. unsalted butter.

Once the butter has melted, add the red onions, garlic, red pepper flakes and salt.

Sauté for 2-3 minutes, until the onion is soft and light brown. Stir often.

Add the crab meat, mayonnaise, half of the nutritional yeast, Italian seasoning, coconut milk, lime juice and spinach. Stir to combine.

Divide the almond flour into two and add half of it to the ingredients in the pot. Stir to combine.

Add the bay leaf.

Cancel the sauté settings.

Close and lock the instant pot lid; set steam release valve to SEALING.

Activate manual high pressure and set cook time to 10 minutes.

Allow 10 to 15 minutes for pressure to build.

Meanwhile, combine the remaining butter, almond flour and nutritional yeast in a small bowl.

After the cooking cycle, release the pressure using the quick release method by turning the steam release valve to VENTING.

Preheat the oven to 450°F.

Open the instant pot lid and discard the bay leaf.

Pour the crab dip into an oven-proof serving dish.

Top the crab dip with the flour mixture and sprinkle the chopped green onions on it.

Place the dish in the oven and bake for 5 minutes, until the topping is browned.

Bring out the dish and serve.

Nutrition:

Calories: 127;

Fat 7.6g;

Carbohydrates: 9.5g;

Fiber: 2.9g;

Protein 6.5g

Artichoke Spinach Dip

Preparation Time: 10 minutes
Cooking Time: 14 minutes + releasing
Servings: 10

Ingredients:

10 ounces frozen spinach bag (defrosted and chopped)
1 can (14 ounces) artichokes (drained and chopped)
1 cup cream cheese (cubed)
2 tbsp. mayonnaise
1 tsp onion powder
2 garlic cloves (minced)
½ cup chicken broth
½ cup sour cream
½ tsp salt
2 jalapeno pepper (diced)
½ cup heavy cream
1 cup grated parmesan cheese
1 cup shredded mozzarella cheese

Directions:

In an instant pot, combine the spinach, artichokes, cream cheese, mayonnaise, sour cream, salt, garlic, jalapeno, onion powder, spinach, artichoke and chicken broth. Stir to combine.

Close the instant pot and set the steam release valve to SEALING. Activate manual high pressure and set the cook time to 4 minutes. Allow 10 to 15 minutes for pressure to build.

After the cooking cycle, release the pressure quickly by turning the steam release valve to VENTING.

Uncover the pot and add the cheeses and heavy cream. Stir until the cheeses have melted.

Serve immediately.

Nutrition:

Calories: 208;
Fat: 16.5g;
Carbohydrates: 8.2g;
Fiber: 2.9g;
Protein: 8.6g

Conclusion

One of the most obvious effects of hormonal imbalance is too much weight gain. People may refer to this as being fat, obese, or just plain overweight. In reality, the food that we eat can alter the balance in the hormones that we have. While there are many factors that could lead to hormonal imbalance like stress, medications, and other environmental factors, the kind of diet an individual has tops it all. Women are more likely to be affected with hormonal imbalance and weight issues. Men and women differ in hormonal composition but it is the latter who suffers more from the effects of weight gain. First of all, women already have a store of body fat due to the presence of estrogen and progesterone. They also have this preference for food with lots of carbs (men prefer meat more). The stress coping mechanism of women is somewhat below that of men. This is the reason why they tend to do stress eating. Women are commonly tasked with cooking and so they tend to eat more.

Even with the scenarios mentioned above, it must be noted that both men and women can be affected by hormonal imbalance problems. Is there a common factor in the statements mentioned above? Yes there is! It is easy to see that food has a big role on how hormones and weight turn out to be. Dieting is the logical solution here. Through the years, different types of dieting techniques have been seen out there. Examples include the no-carbs diet, small-meals diet, liquid-only diet, and many more. Those who used these dieting strategies ended up with a common generalization. None of those things that they did really worked.

The relationship between hormones and weight gain has been established already through researches. It has been found out that when the balance of hormones have been upset, it possible to restore it through a special dieting system. This is the hormone reset diet. This was an innovation conceptualized and developed by Dr. Sara Gottfried. This type of dieting program is anchored on the principle of resetting the seven hormones that are directly related to metabolism. These include insulin, leptin, estrogen, testosterone, thyroid, growth hormone, and cortisol.

It is the body's metabolism that really triggers weight gain. Normally, the food that we eat is converted to energy. During the younger years of an individual, the energy conversion process is quite efficient. More energy is made available for use. This explains why an individual feels he or she has lot of energy for sex, exercise, and other daily activities. However, as the body gets older, the metabolism slows down.

There are substances in the food being eaten that partially contributes to this. In the long run, the body's metabolism gets broken. Under these circumstances, most of the energy from food being eaten is stored within different parts of the body instead of being made available for use in activities. The resulting weight gain and obesity is what weakens the body and gives rise to many symptomatic disorders.

Going back to the mechanism of the hormone reset diet, each of the hormones mentioned above will be "fixed". Three days will be allocated to the resetting of each hormone. This is the minimum number of days needed when resetting the metabolism of the body through hormonal fixes. Dietary changes will be implemented and the main target areas are the gut microbes, liver, and estrogen producing organs.

If seven hormones will be targeted and each reset will take 3 days, the total time to be consumed will be 21 days. This might seem a lot for those who have already tried other crash diet tactics. However, positive results could be seen already on those first 3 days. This means that the entire hormone reset diet approach really works as expected.

Printed in Great Britain
by Amazon